Praise for I

"Raw," "passionate," "real," "overcoming," and "victorious" are just a few words to describe the book you now hold in your hands! My spirit, heart, and personal mirror were transformed as I read the powerful book, *I See Greatness in You,* by my dear friend, Pastor Larry Ragland. I have long believed in the man, but by reading this book I believe even stronger in his burden to love the forgotten. This book is a masterpiece interwoven with pain, triumph, and purpose. It is a message for every person who has ever wondered if God could use the scarred. Larry proves that regardless of the rejection and hurt, our God can use you. Intertwined in these pages are stories that will stir your emotions, but also cause you to arise and confront what has held you back. This book will end the constant "Start Wars" and walk the reader into their divine purpose.

As I have traveled this world ministering to the hurting, my only regret is that I wasn't able to give this book out to the tens of thousands I met who were searching for identity. This book brought one of my favorite Scriptures to mind as I read it: Job 13:15, "Though he slay me, yet will I hope in him; I will surely defend my ways to his face." The theme of this book is simple—it is that the end of yourself is the beginning of God!

One final word to the reader. Never count out the ones that God will use. He always uses the ones that defy man's wisdom and raises up those that he can trust to give him the credit.

—Pat Schatzline

Evangelist and Author, Remnant Ministries International

No matter where you find yourself in life's journey, this book will specifically speak to the greatness in you and powerfully draw that greatness out.

Within the first several chapters I was moved deeply, touched to the point of tears, and inspired by the tremendous plan and awe-amazing destiny that God has for each of us. Larry Ragland's life story, riveting encounters, insight of Scripture, and practical analogies are truly compelling. His willingness to share from the depths of his soul, revealing the moments of true pain and bitterness that life dealt him, will speak to anyone who has ever walked through anything.

In story after story, he shares defining moments of how our heavenly Father overwhelmingly met him during those toughest times with His infinite love and transforming power. Those stories made me also feel that same infinite love God has for me and for every human being.

If you have ever felt hurt, broken, rejected, discarded, or left alone to figure out life, this book will minister to you. Or if you just feel there is more that you were made for, and you just aren't seeing your dreams fully realized, then this book is custom-written for you. It will help you rise above the deep wounds yesterday may have left you with and cause you to soar into a bright, amazing tomorrow.

All of us have greatness in us. That greatness will never fully be realized without addressing and overcoming the enemies of that greatness. This book does exactly that.

—John Smithwick

World Missionary, President and Founder, Global Ventures, Tulsa, OK

I want to recommend Larry Ragland's newest book, *I See Greatness in You*! Larry has been a pastor for over twenty years, where he has excelled at building leaders. He is a dear friend and incredible leader. This book will be mightily used in your life if you give it a try. Use this book like God has used Larry Ragland!

—Scott Dawson

Founder of Scott Dawson Evangelistic Association, Candidate for Governor of Alabama

We rightly seek the truth of God that sets us free within sacred Scripture, and we develop the doctrines that guide our understanding of God, human life, sin, and salvation from the Word of God. However, Pastor Larry Ragland also finds his own life in the Word of God. He sees the hard, often brutal life he suffered within the stories and words of Bible heroes, each of whom was a sinner who suffered at the hands of other sinners. He also found the infinite transforming love of God in Jesus Christ, as well as in his wonderful wife and the other members of the church who loved him even as they loved themselves. Pastor Larry is the recipient of the two great commandments of loving both God and neighbor, and he has allowed that love to turn him into a man who lives out both commandments to love God and so many of his neighbors. I pray that every reader learns these same lessons for their own lives through this wonderful book.

—Fr. Mitch Pacwa, S.J., PhD

Eternal Word Television Network (EWTN)

Host of EWTN Live *and* Scripture and Tradition

I have known Larry for over twenty-five years and I have personally watched a large part of this book unfold in his life. Larry has taken his experiences and woven into his life the stories of those in the Bible who also faced insurmountable odds to become the people God had destined them to be. It's more than one man's story; it is every person's journey, through whatever life has thrown at you, to the place of significance and purpose that God has planned for you.

I See Greatness in You will touch you in places that need to be healed, take you to places that need to be revealed, and from the word of God, empower you to become the greatness God sees in you! The integrity of these pages will reveal the authenticity from which he writes, as well as the power of the principles he shares. It's more than a testimony—it's a tribute to what God can do in and through the lives of those who refuse to remain a victim. And as you read through the chapters, you too, will begin to hear God's voice saying to you, "I See Greatness in You!"

—Frankie Powell

Pastor/Evangelist/Missionary, Pastor and Spiritual Father of Larry Ragland

I have had the distinct privilege of knowing Larry Ragland since his beginning years with Christ and ministry. I've had a close, personal view of his life and journey. However, in this great work, *I See Greatness in You*, Larry opens up so much of his life through a transparency that few are willing to share for the benefit of others. I learned things I never knew about his life because it wasn't yet time to share it. That time has come.

The style in which this book is presented is unique. It weaves thoughts, truths, hopes, and principles in a way that are so connective with all who'll read it. You'll find yourself in these pages in various ways, and you'll be empowered. You'll be pointing to your friends and loved ones to read it. There is Greatness in all of us!

I See Greatness in You will call it out!

—Chris Owensby

Evangelist/Lead Pastor, Grenada, MS

I See Greatness in You!

Unlocking Your Hidden Potential

One Man's Story, Everyone's Journey

LARRY RAGLAND

I See Greatness In You: Unlocking Your Hidden Potential, One Man's Story, Everyone's Journey

This book is dedicated first to the inspiration of my life—my wife and partner, Sandy. Without you, my life would have been a book unwritten. But God sent you into my mess at just the right time. Your words and your love have changed everything about me. You gave me the courage to put the chapters of our life in written form.

Secondly, I dedicate this book to my two beautiful daughters, Elizabeth and Rachel. Only heaven knows all that you endured living the life of a "PK" (pastor's kid). But it was more than that. You helped build and restore multiple church buildings, endured long nights, watched your parents struggle on many levels—over many years. I love you and I am thankful for all you have done and all you continue to do for the kingdom of God.

You make your Daddy proud!

Contents

Foreword		11
A Note from Sandy		13
Preface	Do You See It?	17
Introduction	The DNA of Greatness	19
Chapter One	I See Greatness in You	23
Chapter Two	START Wars	37
Chapter Three	Be Careful What You Ask For	55
Chapter Four	Lessons from a Redwood King	73
Chapter Five	Rubber Band Revelation	93
Chapter Six	Rebuilding the Old Waste Places	115
Chapter Seven	Favor Is Better Than Money	135
Chapter Eight	The Greatest Worst Day	153
Chapter Nine	Double Jubilee	171
Chapter Ten	He Sees Greatness in You!	189

Foreword

I have known Larry Ragland for many years. My father, Fred Stone, was a dear friend of the Ragland family and developed a personal relationship with them over the years. In Larry's first book, *I See Greatness in You*, the reader will discover a testimony from him that reveals extreme levels of physical and emotional abuse. The reader will follow the trail of God's purpose that led to unusual miracles and restoration.

What makes this book unique are the numerous biblical narratives that Larry taps into that conceal powerful and practical spiritual life nuggets that can be applied to the daily life of any follower of Christ. Each reader can discover these truths when reading this book and apply them to their journey with Christ. We overcome the enemy by the blood of Christ and the word of our testimony (Rev. 12:11).

What God has done for Larry He can also do for you!

—Perry Stone Jr.
International Evangelist, Host of "Manna-Fest" Television Program
Director of Voice of Evangelism, OCI and ISOW Bible School

A Note from Sandy

As you read my husband's book, I want to encourage you to open your heart and let it speak to the deepest part of you. I am speaking of the hidden parts that you may have never fully revealed to anyone. Your shame, guilt, lack of self-worth, or intimidation needs to be healed by God. This book will help you, but you must decide at this moment that nothing is going to stop you from finishing the book and the process.

You will be tempted to just put the book down and go on with your life, but my prayer is that you will push through. Larry's story is a story of powerful redemption. It is my story, too. And it is yours.

My Dream

I was only eighteen years old and had recently graduated high school. Only months earlier, I had accepted the proposal to marry the man I loved. Like most girls, I had dreamed of being a wife and mother one day. I had a pretty good idea of what I wanted out of life. It was a dream of a simple home. No drama.

Larry and I graduated from the same high school in a small town. It was the kind of place where just about everyone knew everyone else. So, that meant everyone knew your business! Being a private person, the thought of being the "talk of the town" terrified me. I would've preferred that no one even knew my name. Boy, does God have a sense of humor!

I never imagined that my plan for a "quiet" life would forever be changed in one day. Neither one of us knew what was happening. But as we look back on that moment, we both realize it was the day that changed everything.

Larry had only told me parts of his story. I felt sorry for him; I had seen the pain in his expression when he spoke of the wounds of his childhood. I could only try to relate. My family life was completely different. I had a great relationship with my father. Larry did not. In fact, this void had shaped his entire life. Little did I know, it would shape our entire life too.

The Journey of Greatness

Shame, disappointment, failure, pain, and struggle are all parts of the roadmap to greatness. No one has ever arrived at their purpose without walking through some pain or discomfort. As you read our story, you will also read the stories of many of the most famous Bible characters we know. They are all considered great in the hall of faith! Most would never be called failures. But truthfully, they all failed along the path to greatness.

We have certainly walked through our fair share of struggles, but I would not take anything in exchange for our journey. Just like the characters Larry discusses in this book, we never dreamed our story would be read by the masses. Samson, David, Joseph, and so many others were just living their lives, too. They were trying to survive another day. They didn't have any concept of the greatness within them. The idea that billions would know their story was completely missing from their mind.

Yet they pressed forward. Living life. Pushing through. Failing, learning, falling, and getting back up. These were all building blocks of the greatness within them. And us.

The First Chapter

Chapter one will introduce you to the day that "changed everything" for both of us. It is the foundation for everything we have walked through. It was the cornerstone day that led to the writing of this book thirty years later.

That day, a side of Larry was revealed that I had never known. He had lied to me. The man I loved turned out to be someone I didn't know.

I remember thinking, *I can't do this. This is not what I had planned.*

What happened next affected the rest of our lives. God was working and speaking in an incredible way that day. Two kids in love, clueless of the Big Picture of the moment.

I pray the words of that day become life to you. Let them speak directly to your heart.

Let's Walk Together

We are fully aware that ours is not a story of greatness. It is more of a revelation of the greatness within us all. It is in our DNA, but most never know it is there.

Every chapter of this book will teach you biblical principles about releasing the DNA of the greatness of God within you. I encourage you to take notes, write in the margin of the book, and highlight the passages that speak to your heart. You will be changed. You will be challenged. You will be stretched.

When Larry completed the first draft of this book, I was one of the first to read it. I purposely tried to read it as "Sandy" and not as "Larry's wife." It changed me. It shook me.

My greatest desire is for the same to happen to you. Let's walk through these pages together. Let's find the greatness within.

But let's not stop there. Share the story with others. Most people will never walk in the fullness of their purpose. They just can't see what is inside of them. What they need is someone to help them see it.

People need affirmation and confirmation. They need someone to see what they can't see. That is why God laid it on the heart of my husband to write this. He needed someone to see it. I needed to see it. You need to see it.

I will be the first to say it. Larry will say it over and over throughout the book. God says it in every page of every chapter of the Bible. There is greatness within you! He (God) sees it. I see it too! You need to see it.

Enjoy your journey!

Sandy Ragland

Preface

Do You See It?

I had so many reasons for writing this book. The main reason was me. I needed to get it out of me. I'd been talking about it for years. Other people would say, "Larry, you have to write a book about the experiences of your life. Most people have no idea what you have been through. It will touch people's lives and help them."

I hope that is true. I hope it will help someone face their past, pick up the pieces, and move forward. My dream is that something about my life or the lives of the biblical characters I chose to use can somehow pull the greatness out of you.

But more than anything, this book is a thank-you to all those who helped me find my way. These chapters would not have been possible without you. God used a teenage girl to see greatness in me. He used my children to see a father that I didn't think I could be. God used another man to pastor me, father me, and show me what a man of God looks like.

Father God was a Father to me when my father had dropped me. Ultimately, this book is a big THANK YOU to my true Daddy. He has never left me, rejected me, or dropped me. He has never seen anything but greatness in me, and I am grateful.

He sees greatness in you, too! It's time for you to see it also. Do you see it? You will!

Introduction

The DNA of Greatness

"Then God said, 'Let Us make man in Our image, according to Our likeness; let them have dominion over the fish of the sea, over the birds of the air, and over the cattle, over all the earth and over every creeping thing that creeps on the earth.' So God created man in His own image; in the image of God He created him; male and female He created them" (Genesis 1:26–27).

Mankind was clearly created in the "image" of God, and in His "likeness." God is Good, Love, and Grace personified. He has authority and dominion. Our Father is the complete definition of Greatness. We were created in that image.

In the garden of Eden, man was created to reflect true greatness. God saw greatness in us because He saw Himself in us.

In fact, our Father looked at us and called us (mankind) "very good" (Genesis 1:31). He gave mankind "dominion" over everything on this earth. He saw greatness in us before we could even understand what greatness was.

Most of you are reading this and thinking to yourselves: *Oh, another self-help book on how to be the "best version" of ourselves.* Let me assure you, this is not one of those books.

My heart is to lead us back to our original greatness that can only be found when we see ourselves the way God has always seen us. We are His reflection. Nothing in all of creation can claim this powerful declaration. Angels were not created in His image. Only mankind has the lineage and heritage of our Father. We are His family.

We have all heard people comment on someone else's children: "They look just like you." You may have heard someone say, "You've got your father's nose," or "Your eyes look just like your mother's!" This is because their DNA is in you. In the South (where I am from), we say it this way: "I tell you what, you can't deny him! He is the spitting image of you!"

Inside of every man or woman, regardless of race, creed, nationality, education level or financial status, is the DNA of the eternal God, who created everything in existence. And get this, out of all of it, we are the only thing He ever created in *His image*.

A father's pride is his children. A good father spends time with his kids. He doesn't do this just because he loves them. A good father realizes that one of the most important parts of his role is to make sure his son or daughter knows who they are and what they are capable of. A father is supposed to prepare the children for their life ahead.

Our culture has devalued the role of a father in the home, and society has suffered for it. We now have a generation of young people and adults of all ages who have no idea who they are and who they are supposed to be. The masses are living paycheck to paycheck and struggling to survive. They are living without a revelation of the immense power and authority that is within them. This is because, in many cases, our fathers have not modeled our heavenly Father to us.

Genesis 3:8 tells us that God was "walking in the garden in the cool of the day." Apparently, this was not an uncommon thing for God to do. God enjoyed spending time and talking with His children.

This scripture refers to the first moments after the sin of Adam and Eve. They had just felt the initial consequences of sin. They instantly realized they were naked. They were ashamed.

But God still came for His walk in the garden, like He always did. He called for Adam. Adam replied, "We are behind the bushes. We are hiding because we are naked, and we don't want you to see us this way."

Listen to the words of our Father to the first humans on earth. These words are the foundation of healing to every person who has ever failed.

"Who told you that you were naked?" (Genesis 3:11). You see, God knew exactly what had happened. He knew they were naked and had sinned. But He was, and is, a good Father. He could see greatness in them, even when it seemed impossible to see anything but shame.

Our Father has always seen greatness in us. God can see through mistakes, wrong decisions, toxic environments, even sin; He still sees the greatness in us. He doesn't overlook Adam and Eve; He simply can see beyond them.

I've always looked at this moment in the garden as God's first "altar call." This was an opportunity for man to confess what he had done and admit that he could not make it on his own. Man needs God inside him, on him, and around him. We are doomed to failure without God. The hidden potential inside each of us continues to be covered by our lies and denial.

Over the next few chapters, I have a simple agenda. I want to show you the importance of seeing yourself the way God sees you. I want you to see the greatness inside of you. It is there.

For many, the greatness of our spiritual DNA has been buried by the trials of life. We are overwhelmed by family struggles, finances, health, politics, and even religion. These are tools of our Enemy to "cover" our greatness. Just as Adam and Eve tried to cover themselves and their shame, we are constantly trying to conceal our shame as well. God knew the truth then, and He knows the truth now.

For many, the greatness of our spiritual DNA has been buried by the trials of life.

We are going to look at several people in the Word of God who had times of greatness and times of shame. But there is a reason they are in the Bible. Their stories inspire us, teach us, and convict us to learn from their mistakes and their triumphs.

I will also share stories from my own life that I have never shared publicly before. In fact, many of these moments have only been shared with my wife and my pastor.

I spent the first half of my life never seeing anything great about me or my potential. I needed a father to see greatness in me. Unfortunately, that didn't happen, so my life went in the wrong direction. There may have been destiny and purpose inside of me, but I didn't see it.

I See Greatness In You

You may be just like I was. You are probably saying, "I hear you, Larry, but the truth is, I don't see anything remotely great or even good about me."

You may just need someone to see it in you and call it out of you. I want to be that person for you. I want to call that greatness out of you. I see it. God sees it.

How did I finally begin to see what God sees in me? He spoke into my life in the strangest of times, and in a very unusual way. My prayer for you is that by the time you finish this book, you will see this too and never try to hide from God again. Even if you mess up, you will not quit. Even if you have been dropped and broken by someone you loved and trusted, you will never give up. The greatness within you will not allow it.

The test results are in. Your DNA cannot be denied. Your heritage is one of greatness. Isn't it time you started walking in it?

Chapter One

I See Greatness in You

The VHS Bandit

Standing in a small makeshift courthouse in my hometown's city hall, I heard the words of the judge: "Are you kidding me? What were you thinking?"

The charges were almost laughable, but devastating at the same time. I had rented three VHS tapes, but not returned them. The local video store had me arrested. I was booked and fingerprinted and had my "mugshot" done in the local jail—for three stinking videos!

I suppose I need to explain the "renting of VHS tapes." You see, back in the day, you went to the video store and picked out the movie you wanted to see, and "rented it." The video had to be returned twenty-four hours later or you were charged a late fee. Each day tacked on a new fee. And their motto was: "Be Kind, Please Rewind."

So why didn't I just return the videos? Good question. I guess the answer is the reason I am writing this book! Those videos and that day in the courthouse were a microcosm of my entire life.

The videos had been lying on the back floorboard of my car the entire time. Just like everything else in my life, they were covered up by whatever I could throw in there. I simply forgot about them and moved on. Subconsciously, I guess I thought they would just give them to me and I would never have to pay the bill.

What I didn't realize while I stood there staring at the floor in shame is that less than twenty minutes after the judge's decision, everything in my world would change. I had no idea this was about to happen. In fact, I was standing there thinking the exact opposite of what was about to unfold.

I like to say that this was the first Big Picture moment in my life. I was about to experience a grace and mercy that I had never known. My whole perspective about my self-worth and future life was about to be turned upside down.

This was the beginning of God showing me the Big Picture for my life. His perspective is always different than anything we could ever see. It seems too simple, even cliché, for me to encourage you to find a way to see the Big Picture in your life, but I am convinced it is the key to your purpose and destiny.

You may be tempted to check out of this book at this moment. I can hear some of you saying, "What is so interesting about a twenty-year-old with a misdemeanor record of VHS theft?" I agree; it was a lame way to get my "street cred." This is certainly not a crime novel or a whodunit mystery. But I promise you that if you keep reading, you will see the Big Picture in your own life as well. This is a simple revelation that will change everything.

This is a tale of tragedy, loss, brokenness, abuse, redemption, grace, and purpose! It's God's story. It's mankind's story.

It is a simple revelation that caused me to finally tell the secrets I'd kept silent for the first fifty years of my life.

The Walk of Shame

It has been difficult to revisit many of these moments in my head and heart. I have realized that there is still much brokenness and hurt inside me. I have not completely dealt with all of it. This book has allowed me to bring closure to parts of my past and finally move on. It is not always easy to just "let it go."

This is true for all of us. Just like those videos on the floorboard of my car, we have all thrown an assortment of drugs, sex, money, or even religion over our pain to cover it up. We've just convinced ourselves to forget about it and move on. But you can't move on, because it is still there.

Even though I paid the fine and was released with a misdemeanor offense, the greater offense I had committed was waiting for me outside the courthouse. No, I wasn't going to be picked up by the county sheriff for another crime. In fact, this is the only criminal record I have ever had.

It wasn't *what* that was waiting on me outside; it was *who*.

I had recently started dating the prettiest girl in school. She was way out of my league, and I couldn't believe that she had actually agreed to go out with me. But then, the shocker of all shockers had happened on Christmas Eve: She agreed to marry me! Sandy was barely eighteen years old and had only recently graduated from high school.

She had said yes to a person who was a fraud. She stood in the back of that courthouse and realized for the first time that I had not been honest with her on many levels. She didn't know about any of this.

There was more, too. I had several loans that were in default; my vehicle had been repossessed over a year earlier; and my credit was as low as it could possibly be. I would never be the person with whom Sandy would want to spend the rest of her life.

When the judge said, "You can go," I was relieved, but part of me didn't want to leave. I knew the hardest thing in my life was about to happen. My immaturity, inner demons, and brokenness were about to cost me more than a criminal record. I was about to lose my one shot at the greatest thing to ever happen to me.

As we journey through this book, I want to show you that this is not just my story. This is your story. This story has been lived on various levels by thousands, if not millions, over the years. Some of the greatest Bible heroes lived this life, too. Many were frauds, liars, thieves, adulterers, and even murderers. But God used situations and people in their lives to help them see the Big Picture. They couldn't see it on their own.

God used situations and people in their lives to help them see the Big Picture. They couldn't see it on their own.

The Truth Will Come Out

Most of us have heard the story of Samson. This guy would have been the "jock" of his town. He was in excellent shape and, probably, very popular.

He had been reminded most of his life of the encounter his parents had with the Angel of the Lord regarding his birth. “For behold, you shall conceive and bear a son. And no razor shall come upon his head, for the child shall be a Nazarite to God from the womb; and he shall begin to deliver Israel out of the hand of the Philistines” (Judges 13:5).

The problem with Samson is that he read and believed his own press! He had so much physical strength that he was able to use his gifts to cover up the real man inside. In other words, *his gifts took him places his character couldn't keep him.*

Verse after verse, we read of his strength in battle. But it was never enough. It was almost like he wanted to get caught. He wanted to be exposed.

Later in his life, he meets the now-infamous Delilah. He fell madly in love with her. But she did not love him. She had an ulterior motive. The Philistines were using her to help expose Samson's weakness. The Devil knew the real Samson, even if everyone else did not.

Make no mistake about it. You may have convinced everyone else that you are “OK” or “blessed,” but God knows the real you. Here is a revelation for you. So does the Devil! He is the one who speaks to you in your head and tells you that you can never change. He reminds you of all the words that have been spoken over you. He is there to accuse you, both day and night (Revelation 12:10).

One day, Delilah felt like it was time to expose Samson. She probably put on her prettiest clothes and best perfume, fixed her hair, and got her nails done. She put on some good music and set the mood. When it felt just right, she batted her eyes, smiled, and moved in for the sneak attack.

She pleaded with Samson to tell her the secret of his strength. At first, he lied and said, “If someone binds me with fresh bowstrings that are not dried, I will be as weak as any other man.” She did this, and he woke up and broke the strings. She begged for an answer again, and he proclaimed, “If they bind me with new ropes that have never been used, I will be like any other man.” Of course, after being bound by these, he awoke and broke them, too. But Delilah was persistent. Crying out that he had only lied to her, she pleaded with him to tell her the truth. Then he said, “If you weave the seven locks of my hair into the web of the loom, I will be like any other man.” So she weaved his seven locks tightly into the loom, but Samson once again awoke and broke the tethers (Judges 16:7–14, author's paraphrase).

I believe Samson was at least partially awake during all of this. He was enjoying himself. In his mind, he was indestructible. He was the real-life superhero of the day. Nothing had ever been able to stop him. All his life he had been able to cover up the real Samson with his strength, gifts, and talents. But everything was about to change.

He was so full of himself, he was convinced that he could break every aspect of the Nazarite vow, and still be "Samson—the Man—the Hero of His People."

Each time he told Delilah, "If you do this, I will be like any other man," he convinced himself that he was somehow "not like any other man." His gifts had caused him to think of himself in a way that was not true.

But Samson was indeed just that: a man. He dealt with the same demons that we deal with today.

He finally told her the truth. "If someone shaves my head I will lose all my strength and be like any other man." Of course, while he was lying in her lap, they cut his hair and shaved his head. Samson jumped up and tried to break the ropes, but he could not. He was probably thinking, "This has never happened, something is wrong. I will shake it again, and I'll be OK. I'm always OK." He tried again, and alas, his strength was really gone. He was caught; he was exposed (Judges 16:16–20, author's paraphrase).

He could no longer hide the real Samson from the world. His life had just been turned upside down. He was "like any other man."

I am no Samson, but I know what it feels like to be exposed before the ones you love.

My Greatest Fear

As I walked away from the judge's bench, down a small hallway, and out to the concrete sidewalk, it felt like the longest mile in the world. I knew (as we say in the South) "my chickens had come home to roost." It was all over. No more pretending to be someone I wasn't. The truth is, I had simply become the man that I was told I would be.

We have all been dropped by someone we trust, broken by a tragic event, or believed a lie about ourselves that caused us to stray from the purpose for which we were created.

My childhood and teen years were filled with verbal and physical abuse from my father. For a large part of my life, I was told I was a loser, a failure, and a liar. I was told I would never amount to anything. I would be a "bum." I had been told these things, and at that moment I realized it was all true.

Job said, "For the thing I greatly feared has come upon me, and what I dreaded has happened to me" (Job 3:25).

I had made proclamations over my life like "I will never be like my father" and "I don't care what they say, I will never be what they said I would be." But the truth was that I had become the one person I said I never wanted to be. Inwardly, I always saw myself as a failure. I would never say it with my mouth, but inside I believed it.

Like Samson, I was born with gifts. I never really worked out in a weight room, so my gifts were not tied to physical strength, and certainly not an athletic physique. Since I am a pastor, it made sense that my gift was the gift of gab! I could talk my way out of anything. This meant I was also adept at covering up what was going on inside of me by making people laugh or easily changing the subject. I was even voted "Most Spirited" by my senior class!

My greatest fear was that all my secrets would come out and everyone would know that I was not this funny football player who looked like he had it all together!

He (God) certainly wants the real you to deal with the issues that you keep hiding and covering up.

The truth is that all of us are going to be "arrested" one day. You may never be arrested for something as stupid as not returning three videos, but you will be arrested by the Holy Spirit. He does not want to "punish" you, but He certainly wants the real you to deal with the issues that you keep hiding and covering up.

52,800 Chances to Turn Around

I want you to see a very interesting Scripture about Samson from an earlier part of his life. This was long before he ever met Delilah. Many, or most, skip right over it. Samson was in the desert and he was very thirsty. He has just killed one thousand Philistines with the jawbone of a donkey. He cried out to God for something to drink, and God caused a rock to split and bring forth fresh water.

"So God split the hollow place that is in Lehi, and water came out, and he drank; and his spirit returned, and he revived. Therefore, he called its name En Hakkore, which is in Lehi to this day. And he judged Israel twenty years in the days of the Philistines" (Judges 15:19–20).

Many jump right over the most significant part of that passage: "His spirit returned, and he was revived…And he judged Israel twenty years in the days of the Philistines."

Amid all Samson's inner demons, God revived him. His spirit returned. This means the anointed side of him came back. He judged Israel for twenty years without public embarrassment or rage. But even after twenty years, there was still something inside fighting against his destiny, purpose, and calling.

The Bible goes on to say that after twenty years: "One day Samson went to Gaza, where he saw a prostitute. He went in to spend the night with her" (Judges 16:1 NIV).

After twenty years with no issues, one day he decides to throw it all away! He just gets up and starts walking toward Gaza. He knew what was there. He knew why he was going. It was almost as if he had to do this to finally satisfy his tormented inner man. It was a path the Enemy had planned out to destroy Samson, to destroy God's man.

It reminds me of the famous quote: "Those who fail to learn from history are doomed to repeat it." If you do not deal with the past and the hidden issues inside you, they will deal with themselves for you. You can deny and push them aside all you want; but, like Samson, one day you will get up and start heading down the path of exposure.

I remember the old-time preachers from my childhood, saying, "You better clean those closets, or the Lord will clean them for you." That may be a little hard-line for some of the people in the church; but the truth is – the truth cannot stay hidden! It will always come out: either by choice or by force.

When Samson started towards Gaza, he knew it was approximately twenty-five miles from his home. Gaza was the capital of the Philistines. He was headed straight for the most fortified and heavily armed area of the nation. He was begging for someone to confront him. His intention was to go straight to the red-light district and find a prostitute. He was a man on a mission.

Whatever you do, don't miss this next point. We know twenty-five miles is a long walk, but did you know that it comes to 52,800 steps? Samson had 52,800 chances to turn around. Samson didn't get up one day and decide to ruin his life. Those twenty-five miles were in him before he ever started walking.

In reality, he had been walking toward that moment most of his adult life. Every day that passed without dealing with the inner truth of the real Samson was another step towards destruction. Just like Samson, people don't ruin their lives overnight. Most people don't decide to leave their spouse on a whim. No, they make a series of choices. They allow themselves to be in situations they know they shouldn't be. Or they have allowed outside voices to speak into them, planting seeds of doubt in themselves or their spouse.

Samson had twenty-five miles to change his mind. Many of you have been walking for years in the wrong direction. You have convinced yourself that if you just keep walking, you will finally get far enough away that no one will even notice you.

As Low as You Can Go

I remember it like it was yesterday. I have told this story many times. Other than when I surrendered my life to Christ, this was the most important day of my life. It changed everything.

I was prepared for the worst. I played the scenes through my head at lightning speed. It only took a couple of minutes to walk outside. But I had already run fifty possible scenarios through my head of what was about to transpire. Unfortunately, all of them ended badly.

They all concluded with Sandy walking away. Come on, why would anyone want to stay?

I decided to suck it up and just set her free. She deserved better than me anyway. I couldn't shake who I was. Just like Samson, I could stay focused for a long time, but the old Larry always came out eventually. It was just who I was.

We quietly walked a few more steps and stopped on the sidewalk in front of city hall. I was shaking on the inside. At that moment, I was a little boy again, wanting desperately to be affirmed, only to be rejected. I was sure my destiny would be rejection again. I deserved it. This time, I really deserved it. I mentally prepared myself for it.

Samson Sees the Real Samson

Samson was imprisoned and made to grind meal like a donkey for the Philistines. They didn't really need him to do that job; it was for their enjoyment. They wanted to see him lowered to the state of an animal. His eyes had been gouged out, and his head was kept shaven. He was spat on, beaten, and mocked.

The same man that had once ripped a lion into pieces, carried an iron city gate on his back, and single-handedly defeated thousands of soldiers was now walking in a circle tied to a millstone. He had hit rock bottom. He probably played out in his head thousands of scenarios of how this would end for him. They all ended badly.

The great Samson was now entertainment for the higher classes of Philistia. His inner struggle had finally turned him into the failure every one of his enemies so desperately desired him to be.

But they were not through embarrassing him. When they were having a feast, they tied him to the two center columns of the great banquet hall, where everyone who was anyone would be eating that night. They would be making a sacrifice to their false god, Dagon. It would be the highlight of the evening. They made him perform and dance for them.

The once-undefeated giant of a man would be put in a place of total exposure. I am sure people would hit him, spit on him, and curse him. But he was blind; he couldn't see them. He couldn't see anything. But he could still see himself.

Samson had always seen himself with his natural eyes. I can imagine a person as conceited as him checked out his reflection in any glass or bit of water that presented itself to see what a great man he was. But all along, God desired for him to see himself through the eyes of God.

Chained to the columns, unable to see himself in the natural, Samson finally saw himself in the Spirit.

God had seen the real Samson before his parents even knew he would ever exist. The Angel of the Lord told his mother, who was barren and could not have a child, that she would give birth to a great man! God saw the real Samson before there was a Samson. God is the Big Picture!

Think about this: Any time Samson is ever portrayed in a movie, painting, or any likeness, he is always very muscular. I tend to believe he probably wasn't as "ripped" as we have thought. Now don't get me wrong! I am sure that he was not scrawny or overweight, but his strength never came from his muscles. *His strength came directly from God.*

Chained to the columns, unable to see himself in the natural, Samson finally saw himself in the Spirit. I believe at that moment, he got a revelation of the Big Picture. He finally saw what his life was really all about.

I think he realized that all that power had been "gifted" to him for the glory of God and for his people. It had never been about him. It was supposed to be used for others. He was called to lead and protect God's people in Israel. He was basically called to be a pastor and leader to the people.

In that moment, he remembered a part of the story his parents had told him. In all his exploits and fame, he had allowed himself to forget about the Angel of the Lord's message regarding his life. He was so consumed with being "the man," he forgot his prophesied destiny: "And he shall begin to deliver God's people from the hand of the Philistines" (Judges 13:5, author's paraphrase). In his blindness and shame, Samson remembered his purpose!

Five Words

Sandy and I were standing right on the edge of the sidewalk. I'm sure people were walking around us. Cars were moving back and forth on the small-town street. But I didn't notice any of it. I was trying to look at her for as long as I could. I didn't know if I would ever see her again. She was, and still is, the most beautiful creation of God I've ever seen. Surely this was it for us.

She was a very shy girl back then, and a person of few words. In that moment, she wasn't saying anything. So I broke the awkward silence.

I said, "Sandy, I want you to go. You deserve so much better than me. I am not the man you thought I was. I have lied to you and deceived you. I promise you I will never speak badly of you. I want you to be happy. So, please just walk away. I completely understand, and I will never hold it against you." I prepared for the goodbye.

When I think back to what happened next, I realize that this was a kingdom of God moment for me. This was a moment when God allowed me to hear from someone else what He sees in me.

What was her response? What words would come out of her mouth?

Those words changed my life and are the reason I am writing this book today. Sandy said, "I'm not leaving. I'm not going anywhere." I immediately replied, "Sandy, you heard and saw what just happened. I've not been honest with you on many levels. Why would you ever stay with me?"

Five words. Her response was, "I see greatness in you!" No one had ever said those words to me. Five words that could not be unheard in my spirit or my mind. Five simple words that took a fraud and a fake, and made him believe that he could do something great. Five words that I have repeated to my children, my church, and so many others. The Bible says, "Death and life are in the power of the tongue" (Proverbs 18:21a). Those five words had life in them, like nothing that had ever been spoken to me. Five words from an eighteen-year-old girl would be the foundation for the journey that we would take together.

> Those five words had life in them, like nothing that had ever been spoken to me.

Can you imagine? Twenty years of doubt, and twenty years of fear, were crushed with just five words. I am convinced that each one of us needs to hear those five words from someone.

All my life, my mother had told me that I could be anything I wanted to be. She had always tried to instill confidence in me. Mama was always there for me. She fought for me and my brother and provided for us. My mother is a great mother!

But there was something about that moment that moved from the physical realm and went right into my spirit man. I could feel that something had changed in me. God had called us both to do something great. She used her mouth to say the words, but it was God that spoke through her.

I've asked Sandy many times, "What did you see in me to make you say that?" She always says, "It was just God. At that moment, I saw it in your eyes. I knew it was God, and I was supposed to be with you."

Strength versus Greatness

Samson was chained to the columns in shame. He could not see himself, or anyone, or anything. But for the first time in his life, something rose up inside him. It wasn't strength. It was greatness!

From the beginning, God had called him to be greater than his enemies, but Samson hadn't been able to find peace in that alone. He had continued to dwell with his enemies and allowed them to speak into his life. He allowed the Enemy to identify him; now the Enemy had him in chains. It was all a part of Satan's plan to destroy God's man before he completed his destiny.

"Then Samson prayed to the Lord, 'Sovereign Lord, remember me. Please, God, strengthen me just once more, and let me with one blow get revenge on the Philistines for my two eyes'" (Judges 16:28 NIV).

My paraphrase: Samson cried out to God, "Will you see greatness in me one more time? I can't see, for I am blind, but You can be my eyes. I want to finally see what You see." God replied, "I've always seen greatness in you. Now you finally see it. You now know the purpose for which you were created. Samson, *push*!"

Ironically, it was the last few minutes of Samson's life that exposed him to the Big Picture. This moment revealed to him the reason he was born. For the first time in his life, he didn't think of himself. His prayer for one more moment of greatness was not for him; it was for his people. He realized that in that one act, he would kill more of the enemies of God's people than he had in all his years of doing it his way.

"And Samson took hold of the two middle pillars which supported the temple, and he braced himself against them, one on his right and the other on his left. Then Samson said, 'Let me die with the Philistines!' And he pushed with all his might, and the temple fell on the lords and all the people who were in it. So the dead that he killed at his death were more than he had killed in his life" (Judges 16:29–30).

Samson found his greatness. He realized it was never possible for him to be everything he was destined to be *on his own*. Samson finally understood that his identity was not in the way the villagers praised him for his mighty acts of strength. In the end, he realized that all the beautiful women in the world would never complete him and give him a sense of worth. No! At that moment, Samson realized there was only one thing that mattered—and that was who God said he was!

I want to be your Sandy. I want to look you in the eye and tell you, "I see greatness in you." I know it is there because God put it there.

You will read story after story about how God slowly revealed Himself to me. His hand has always been on me. His hand is on you as well. Greatness is in there. It is hidden. We are going to pull it out!

I want to look you in the eye and tell you, "I see greatness in you." I know it is there because God put it there.

I See Greatness In You

With your mouth, say these words right now: "God, I know there is greatness in me. No matter what I've done, or said, there is greatness in me. No matter what has been done to me, or said to me, or about me—I know there is greatness in me." Shout it aloud! "I know there is greatness in me!" Now, let's get started.

Chapter Two

START Wars

Heartbreak Hotel

In the 1950s, you didn't just leave your husband. My mother was taught to make it work out: No matter what the man did, just be a good wife to him and it will all work out in the end.

I've heard the story of their wedding night many times. Mama was watching her lifelong favorite singer on a small black-and-white TV. Of course, this was not just any singer. This was the King of Rock and Roll: Elvis Presley.

It didn't matter that every young lady swooned over him anytime they saw him. No, that night, it was supposed to be all about her husband.

When he found her watching and singing along with Elvis, he was filled with jealousy. My father physically hit my mother that night. This was the first time physical abuse came into her life. It would certainly not be the last. A foundation of intimidation, insecurity, doubt, violence, and abuse began on their wedding night.

The foundation of any building is the most important part of its construction. The house may be beautiful, even feel safe, for a few years, but the "hidden" problems will always show up. They will begin as a small crack, but quickly lead to bigger damage.

Eventually, the foundational problems begin to work their way through the entire house. Doors do not shut correctly. Sheetrock begins to separate at the joints. Strange noises and loud popping sounds occur, as the entire structure begins to sink and settle.

False Start

The reason I call this chapter "START Wars" is twofold. One, I am a HUGE movie buff, and it's just a cool play on the name of one of the greatest movie franchises ever made. And two, I have come to realize that the war for our souls, is at its strongest, at the START. Let me explain.

The Bible says, "Being confident of this, that he who began a good work in you will carry it on to completion until the day of Christ Jesus" (Philippians 1:6 NIV).

The key word in this verse is "began." It seems simple, but for some reason we don't really understand the power of that statement. We are supposed to be "confident" in the process. He doesn't just promise to be there at the beginning. He also promises us that He will "carry it on to completion," or until the end!

Our Father will *never* stop doing everything He can to pull the real "you" out of you. Our Father is relentless in His pursuit of us. Even though He is sitting on a heavenly throne, and not physically here on earth with us, He is not an absent father. He is with us through everything we experience, both good and bad.

Paul said he was confident in this premise. I would paraphrase it this way: "God will finish what *He* starts, not necessarily what *we* start." Therein lies the problem. We expect God to finish what we start. But He only promised that He would carry to completion what *He* started.

I've heard it said, "If the ladder is not leaning against the right wall, every step we take just gets us to the wrong place faster." It really matters where you place that ladder. The journey does not begin when you start climbing the ladder; the true beginning started when you placed the ladder against the wall.

You may know the story of Moses and how God used him to lead the children of Israel out of bondage from the Egyptians. (We'll cover his amazing birth and the remarkable events that led to him becoming the liberator of his people in the next chapter.) But for now, let's talk about the Exodus from Egypt.

What I want you to see is the "way" God brought them out at the beginning of their journey. The Bible describes the condition in which God "started" their journey to freedom. "He brought out Israel, laden with silver and gold, and from among their tribes no one faltered." (Psalms 105:37 NIV).

In one day, they went from being slaves to being covered with silver and gold. There was literally not one sick person in the nation. God healed every disease, pain, and sickness. There were no cripples. There were no blind people; there were no infirmities at all.

And yet, after only a couple of weeks, they started griping and complaining about their conditions. They were rich, healed, and had just witnessed God's display of love for them on a level no human being had ever seen. The truth was that *God had brought them out of Egypt, but they still had Egypt in their hearts.*

God had brought them out of Egypt, but they still had Egypt in their hearts.

Moses and God were trying to show them they were free, but they only saw themselves as slaves. That is all they had ever known. Their foundation was severely cracked. Their self-confidence and identity had been defined by the taskmasters of Egypt instead of Father God.

In less than three weeks, they found themselves stopped at the Red Sea. Mountains and deserts were on each side of them, and Pharaoh was pursuing from behind. (He quickly changed his mind about letting them go.)

You would think they would begin to shout, "I can't wait to see what God is about to do!" Instead they said, "'Is this not the word that we told you in Egypt, saying, "Let us alone that we may serve the Egyptians"? For it would have been better for us to serve the Egyptians than that we should die in the wilderness'" (Exodus 14:12).

Can you imagine? Their words to Moses were, "It would have been better to stay and *serve* the Egyptians!" The Devil had created a foundation of slavery in them. They called slavery—serving!

They believed there was no other way for them. Defeat was their identity, and no amount of gold or silver would change that. Healing and miracles could not change the foundation. It was a matter of the heart.

They had "started" out in bondage, and in their minds, they left Egypt in bondage. They had mentally convinced themselves that slavery was better than their current situation. This is the tool of the Enemy.

The war is at the start.

They put the ladder of their freedom against the wrong wall. God will provide us the ladder to freedom, but we have to make sure we are trying to climb over the right wall.

God will provide us the ladder to freedom, but we have to make sure we are trying to climb over the right wall.

I spent most of my life climbing higher but getting nowhere. I couldn't figure out why it seemed so hard to escape the past and move beyond the things that were said and done to me and my family. But I finally realized I was never going to make it to the top of that ladder. I had the wrong ladder, and I had the wrong wall.

Subconsciously, I was asking God to complete what I started. I had decided I could figure this out on my own. I always thought that my personality or talents would be enough to get me out of any situation. But just like any bad foundation, inevitably it began to crack, and I began to sink and settle.

8 mm Memories

For years, my mom had tried to have a child. She desperately needed someone to love, someone who would love her back with unconditional love. At long last, at age twenty-nine, she gave birth to a 10.5 lb. boy—me. Ironically, I was born on Elvis Presley's birthday.

She has told me so many times about how big my feet were. She said they were so big that the nurses from other floors were coming down to see them. As a pastor, I have used that story many times. I like to say that those were "Devil-stomping feet," even at birth!

I have been told that for a brief season of my newborn life, things were good. My dad seemed to be happy with me in his life. I have seen some old, grainy 8 mm films of me running around the house with my Dad chasing after me, laughing. I was probably around two years old at that time. Sadly, I have no idea where those home movies are today. They are simply grooves carved in my mind, only to be replayed by me.

But things quickly changed. Without even realizing what had happened to me, the ladder was moved.

Honestly, I don't have a lot of great memories from my life with my father. I do have some, but they are very few. Most of the images in my mind are of the countless times I did so many different things to try and win his love and affirmation. But I never felt like I received it.

Disclaimer

At this point I need to say this. I did not write this book to bash my father by telling stories that make you cry. My experiences with my dad are central to my story of healing and to helping you find your hidden greatness. I believe they will touch you and give you hope in knowing that if God can do something with my life, He can certainly do something amazing with yours.

Double-Barrel Moment

Everyone has what we call "monumental moments." These events so impact our lives that we remember them vividly for many years to come, even the rest of our lives.

One such moment happened when I was in middle school around the age of ten. My mother and father were fighting like normal. Honestly, I don't remember what it was all about or what was even said. But I distinctly remember my mother telling us "to get in the car because we were leaving for good."

I was only ten. I had begged my mother to leave him on many occasions, but truthfully, I wanted it to work out. I wanted my family to be together. I really loved my dad and simply wanted to believe that he loved me and was proud of me.

He knew I was tenderhearted in this area. He knew that he could influence my emotions and use them to control me and the situation. As my younger brother and I were preparing to get in the car, something happened that would scar me for many years to come. My father left the room and then returned. When he came back, he held a double-barrel 12 gauge shotgun in his hands.

I knew the shotgun. I had seen it before. I think he had even let me shoot it once. He was screaming and cursing. Suddenly he yelled at me and told me to look at him. I was terrified. I didn't know what was about to happen.

He made me watch him load it. He turned the gun around and pointed the barrel towards his face. He grabbed my hand and forced my fingers onto the trigger. I was shaking uncontrollably. He then said words that have stayed with me my entire life: "Son, kill me. Pull the trigger. Blow my brains out. Because if you let your mother leave, that's what I am going to do to myself. So you might as well kill me now, because it is the same. It will be your fault either way."

The False START

A controlling spirit gets its strength from making the person who is being controlled think its effect is actually their fault. This has been the plan of the Enemy from the very beginning.

Life is a race. Paul said, "Do you not know that those who run in a race all run, but one receives the prize? Run in such a way that you may obtain it" (1 Corinthians 9:24).

A controlling spirit gets its strength from making the person who is being controlled think its effect is actually their fault.

Run in such a way to win! To win a race takes training, discipline, and the right attitude. Each race is different. Marathons take endurance and the right pace to finish. Relays require great teammates and coordination. Some races are sprints; they are "all-out running with everything you got" for just a few seconds. But all races have two things in common. They all have a start, and they all have a finish.

The START Wars principle is this: "The way you see yourself at the *start* of the race will affect how you see yourself during the tough parts of the race." The course of each race is different. It looks one way on a map, but it is an entirely different experience when you actually run it.

For instance, marathons take you through busy cities, down country roads, up steep hills, and through various climates. You can easily map out the course on paper or on your smartphone. You can train twenty-six miles every day to prepare for the marathon, but the conditions will be different on the day of the race. Preparation is more than running; it is also mental and spiritual.

> The way you see yourself at the *start* of the race will affect how you see yourself during the tough parts of the race.

Many races are won and lost at the *start*. If you are in a sprint race and you "jump the gun," you can be disqualified. If you have a slow start, you will probably not win. The start is extremely important.

God started this world right. Everything He made and created, He called good. After He made man, He stepped back, looked at it all, and thought, "it was very good" (Genesis 1:31). In fact, God has never made anything bad. Everything He has ever made is good.

The problem has never been with the Designer of the course or race. The issue is with the runners. We are the ones who continue to have a false start. We jump the gun and get ahead of God all the time.

Many times, people blame God for the problems of their lives. "How could this have happened? What kind of God would allow that in our world?" But God made the world and it was good. Man was the one who messed it up.

Remember, we had the greatest start of all creation. We had more going for us than any animal, plant, or even angel. We were the *only* part of creation that *started* out looking just like God, our Father. We were created in His image. We were covered in His glory. We walked with

Him in the garden. We had one-on-one conversations with Him. There is no better start than that!

But over the course of time, man began to listen to another voice. That voice was the voice of the Enemy of God and man. Satan began to say things like, "What did God really say about this tree?" Eve gave her reply to the serpent. Satan then stated, "Well, let me tell you what He really meant…"

This was an attempt to convince man that he needed a "restart." He appealed to the side of man that wanted to chart his own course. Satan was letting them know, "You can be just like God if you eat from this tree. That's why He doesn't want you to eat the fruit."

The lie of the Enemy and the tragic "false start" of that moment made Adam and Eve forget that they were already like God! Man was created in God's image.

At the moment they took of the fruit and ate, their eyes were opened. They knew they were naked. They had just chosen to start their own race. They had moved the ladder.

The irony of it all is that Satan tried to convince them they were missing out on something. The liar was accidentally telling them the truth with his lie. Because of God's glory, they were missing out on sickness, poverty, loneliness, depression … the list goes on and on.

I've heard it said, "One act of disobedience ruined the world for the rest of us."

Listen, there is no way the decision to eat of the fruit that day was a spur-of-the-moment choice. That event was the result of a process that "started" a long time before that actual moment. Somewhere along the way, a seed of doubt was allowed to be planted in their hearts, and it grew to a sinful decision that changed history.

The Coal Miner Hero

My mother was so distraught at my condition, as I stood trembling with my hand on the trigger of the shotgun, that she screamed, "OK, we will stay!"

Of course, my dad promised to change once and for all this time. We went to the station wagon, got our stuff, and brought it back in the house.

Everything was pretty good for a while. Then it all started again. But this time, it grew worse. This is the way abusers are to their victims. They promise the moon in the heat of the moment, but as soon as they feel like you are securely back, they return to their old ways. But – just like an addict – the next time the drug must be stronger for the same effect. The abuser must be meaner, or more threatening, to feel like they have achieved their goal.

One day I was playing in the yard with some of my cousins. It was the middle of summer in Alabama. That means humidity you can literally feel in the air. It will almost choke you at times. Like most boys my age, in that kind of heat, I had my shirt off.

I can remember that day well. It had been a good day; it was a fun day. That is, until I had another moment with my father.

We were playing army in the yard, and my dad was working on some project outside in the driveway. He had pulled some carpet up from the floor, and several pieces were lying on the ground. Like I had done many times before, I asked him if I could help him. I wanted so badly to feel like my father needed me. I would do whatever I could to try and show him my desire to learn the things he knew. I just wanted him to teach me how to be a man.

Much to my surprise, he said, "Sure, come here and let me show you how to do this." I was so excited. I told my cousins I couldn't play anymore. I was my dad's helper now!

Up until that day, I don't remember my dad trying to teach me any "guy things." But today was a new start for us. We were going to be father and son working on a project together. That is, until I messed up slightly, and he said, "I knew you couldn't do this. I don't know why I even told you to help me." I was devastated. I began to cry. He said, "Be a man and wipe those tears from your face. Go back and play, and let me finish this."

It was like I had an out-of-body experience. I feared my father greatly, but at that moment I yelled at him and said something I won't repeat now. He was shocked.

Honestly, I don't remember all of the words I said that day. But I do remember that I cursed at him. I used some of the words that he had used against me on many occasions.

It enraged my father. He picked up one of the pieces of carpet and began to hit me across my bare back with the backside of the carpet. He knocked me down the hill, then chased me and hit me again. Fear gripped my heart. I ran as hard as I could run.

I ran straight to my grandparent's house at the bottom of the hill. When I ran in the house, I was obviously shaken. I think I was a little bloody from contact with the rough backing of the carpet, or maybe from the falls, but it was apparent that something major had happened. When my grandfather saw me, something came over him that I had never seen in him before.

He was a legend in my eyes and in the eyes of many in our little town. He had worked in the coal mines most of his life. He was a farmer and a blacksmith, and he raised pigs. He even had his own shack in which he repaired watches and guns for people all around us. It was common to see strangers there several days a week, waiting for him to do something for them. We were all enamored of him.

My grandfather had a wild streak in him, too. Sometimes he would go out with the boys and be gone for a few days. Then he would be back, sober and hard at work. He may have been rough around the edges, but he loved his grandkids. Grandmother and Granddaddy were everything to me and my cousins.

That day, he took one look at me, and he ran (the best he could) up the hill. I was still very upset, but running right behind him. He made it to our house, and my father was still working outside. He looked at my father, and said, "Let me tell you something: If you ever touch my grandson again, I will kill you." My dad replied, "Now, settle down and listen…" That's all he got out of his mouth before my grandfather knocked him out with one punch. He was out like a light!

My emotions were all over the place. On the one hand, I was ecstatic to see him finally have someone stand up to him. On the other hand, I loved my father and hated to see that happen to him. Plus, I truly feared what would happen to me and my grandfather once my father came to himself again. Surprisingly, he never said a word back to Granddaddy, and he didn't mention the event to me.

The Blame Game

"And He [God] said, 'Who told you that you were naked? Have you eaten from the tree of which I commanded you that you should not eat?' Then the man said, 'The woman whom You gave to be with me, she gave me of the tree, and I ate.' And the Lord God said to the woman, 'What is this you have done?' The woman said, 'The serpent deceived me, and I ate'" (Genesis 3:11–13, insertion mine).

This was the launch of the START Wars. What happened at the beginning truly affects the rest. This is a bedrock principle of God's Word. Without the birth (start) of Christ, there could be no death on the cross. Without the cross (the start of the New Testament), there could be no resurrection. Without the resurrection, there could be no Pentecost. Without Pentecost, there could be no church. Without the church, we could not spend eternity with God.

God speaks directly to the serpent. "So the Lord God said to the serpent: 'Because you have done this, you are cursed more than all cattle, and more than every beast of the field; on your belly you shall go, and you shall eat dust all the days of your life. And I will put enmity between you and the woman, and between your seed and her Seed; He shall bruise your head, and you shall bruise His heel" (Genesis 3:14–15).

Most of the things you are going through right now were not caused by the Devil.

If you want to walk in the unseen greatness that God has placed within you, it is time to stop blaming everyone in the world for your problems. Most of the things you are going through right now were not caused by the Devil. Many of them are a result of your own choices, actions, and words. Still others are a direct result of how you "started out" seeing yourself as a young person: in the beginning.

God knew man would play the "blame game" from the beginning. In Revelation 13:8b we see something very interesting. Jesus is proclaimed to be "the Lamb slain from the foundation of the world." Note that it says He was slain "from" the foundation of the world. He knew He would have to die before He ever said, "Let there be light."

The start is so important. It is amazing to me that God did not say to the serpent, "A man or a prophet or a teacher is coming who will crush your head." No, He said there is a "Seed" coming from a woman.

The Devil was laughing at Eve's decision, which would ultimately change the world. He thought that he had won. But God spoke directly to the serpent and said, "A Seed will come forth from a woman in the future that will destroy you!" (My paraphrase.)

The War in Bethlehem

I love to spend time teaching about the garden of Eden. I truly believe it is the cornerstone to understanding the heart of God. It is God's perfect will. This world was started right.

Just read the first few chapters of Genesis and the last couple of chapters of Revelation, and you will see the similarities. God's plan for His kids has never changed. When Eve took of the fruit and gave it to Adam, it did not shock God. He is all-knowing. He knew creation would not be able to remain perfect. He was not caught off guard. He had a plan before the garden was ever planted.

The whole gospel begins with the prophecy in the garden. When God said to the serpent, "There is a Seed coming," it was a direct prophecy of the birth of Christ. In one verse, God spelled out the entire plan. The birth of Jesus Christ would truly change the world.

The whole gospel begins with the prophecy in the garden.

When Christ was born, the world literally stopped counting years and started over! It was a new START on every level. Jesus did not come to destroy the Law and all the teaching of the past. He clearly said He came to fulfill it all. He didn't take away the need for a lamb; He became the Lamb (see John 1:29). He didn't stop requiring a priest to stand before us and God; He became our one and only Priest (see Hebrews 4:14). The requirement for blood to cover our sins was not removed; Jesus shed His blood once and for all—for all mankind (see Hebrews 10:19).

I could go on and on. The birth of Jesus didn't reboot humanity and start over with a new creation. He just moved the ladder to the right wall. He dug up the damaged foundation and replaced the cracked block with Himself. Jesus became the Chief Cornerstone (see Ephesians 2:20).

Several years ago, I wrote a short story called "The War in Bethlehem." It has since been read all over the world and translated into other languages. It has touched many hearts because it gives us a new look at the events we celebrate at Christmas. It reveals that it was more than a birth; it was a culmination of a war in the heavens that had been fought for thousands of years.

When Satan heard the prophecy of the coming Seed of the woman, he set out to immediately prevent it. Lucifer is not God. He is not all-knowing. Therefore, he didn't fully understand what it all meant. In his mind, he thought it would probably be the next man after Adam.

Satan is not a Big Picture kind of guy; he is a Little Picture being (more on that in the coming chapters). But for now, let's just say that Satan is impatient and will never be able to know exactly what's going on in the master plan of the moment. What is the next story we read about after the fall of man and this prophecy of Satan's coming doom? The story of Cain and Abel.

The Devil immediately went after the next seed of the woman: Cain. He thought, "If I can mess him up, I will stop the plan." Over time, he was able to infiltrate Cain's heart, filling it with his own heart. Jealousy, pride, and rage consumed Cain until he rose up and killed his brother Abel.

Even though Cain did not die in the physical, he died in the spiritual. In one day, Satan took out any chance that the next two seeds of the woman would ever crush his head. It was over in his mind. But mankind continued to be fruitful and multiply, and before long, entire nations existed. Thousands and then millions of people began to fill the land. Satan was in a panic. Which one was the Seed?

He decided to kill every "God-Man" that ever appeared, so that any time a prophet appeared, he had a bull's-eye on him. One by one they were killed, tortured, and imprisoned. Each one was suspected of being the coming Messiah.

"But when the fullness of the time had come, God sent forth His Son, born of a woman, born under the law" (Galatians 4:4).

When Jesus came into this world, He was preceded in birth by His cousin, John the Baptist. John would later be revealed as the fulfillment of the prophecy of the forerunner of Christ. He was the one whom the prophets had foretold would pave the way for the ministry of the Messiah. He, too, was brutally killed, like so many prophets before him.

The story of Christmas is so much more than a baby being born in a small cave filled with livestock and hewn from the mountains of Bethlehem. Many things were going on that day in the natural—and certainly in the spiritual. This was a war being fought for mankind. This war was fought for the greatness inside God's children. The unseen greatness God had placed in man from the beginning, which had been subsequently lost on that fateful day at the tree in the garden, hung in the balance.

The unseen greatness God had placed in man from the beginning, which had been subsequently lost on that fateful day at the tree in the garden, hung in the balance.

Here is an excerpt from the final few paragraphs of my story, "The War in Bethlehem":

> This was the greatest war ever fought in the history of eternity. God's angels were fighting the Devil's angels by the multiplied trillions. Mighty warring angels were fighting with everything they had to stop the demons of hell from getting to this precious woman riding on a donkey.
>
> I can hear the angels of God, crying out to each other with words of encouragement, "Hold on! Just a little while longer and it will be over." The angel looks down through the clouds and sees that someone has given Mary a place to lay.
>
> The battle intensifies; it's getting closer. The pains of labor have set in. Mary is breathing deeper and has now begun to cry

out in the travail of birth. She didn't think that it would be this hard to give birth to a child that had been conceived by the Holy Ghost Himself.

Thank God, she's not alone. She has the love of her life, Joseph, kneeling next to her, encouraging her the entire way. He could have left her, but he didn't. She has a godly man, who will not leave her or Jesus.

The pains are now greater and the warfare in the heavens is greater as well. All of hell is unleashed for its final barrage. God's angels are ready! The Father sends reinforcements. The mighty warring angels of God are called up to the battle.

Down on earth it is becoming almost unbearable for Mary. She is not only facing the normal pain of childbirth; she is trying to give birth to a baby that trillions of fallen angels are fighting to kill.

Then suddenly, Joseph shouts, "Don't give up! I see Jesus!" Mary is encouraged and gives a final push.

At that moment, there is a silence that seems to last an eternity. The soldiers stop fighting. Both sides are waiting to see what just happened.

A sound begins to echo in the cave and out of the mountain. This sound emanates through the streets and into the heavens. What was that sound? The sound of a baby crying. The sound of a perfect child being born. The sound of victory! The sound of the Seed of the woman. The prophecy was fulfilled! The battle had been won! Jesus was born!

The Bible tells us that at that moment a "host" of angels began to sing. The word "host" in the original language is defined as "army." This was a victory chorus sung by heavenly soldiers who had been fighting and pushing towards this moment for thousands of years. The warring angels, created to fight, heard the sweet sound of that baby's cry for the first time. It was the cry of total victory!

What did this battalion sing? Luke tells us: "Glory to God in the highest, and **on earth peace**, good will toward men" (Luke 2:14; emphasis mine).

A computer is programmed to do amazing things that cannot be comprehended by our finite minds. Yet, these amazing machines still manage to lock up and make us want to throw them out the window. Sometimes the only thing that can bring that computer back to its greatness is to simply reboot the machine.

When Jesus came into this world through the womb of the Virgin Mary, the reboot happened. Man was given the opportunity for greatness again!

"Why Didn't You Finish?"

My family lived on a small sloping hill with several of my cousins. My grandparents lived at the bottom of the hillside. Granddaddy had bought the whole area many years ago and had divided it among most of his children. This meant I was assured an exciting childhood of building forts, playing army, and various sports with my cousins.

Each of my mother's brothers and sisters were given sizable areas of land to call their own. My mom was given just under two acres of property. It was a lot of grass to cut. We didn't have a riding mower, so it meant the grass was usually cut in stages so we wouldn't die of heatstroke.

One particular day of grass cutting would change my life forever. It seemed like any other hot and humid day. It was in the middle of the summer, and my father had told me to make sure I got it all cut. I remember feeling determined to have it all finished for him. I started early, drank a lot of water, and kept going. I didn't stop for food. I was going to finish this and make my father proud of me!

I cut grass for hours, until I could not stand any longer. There was only one patch left, under a few large pine trees that you couldn't see unless you walked down into that area. I thought, *He will not see that, and I will finish it tomorrow.* I went inside just a few minutes before I knew he would be home from work.

I distinctly remember collapsing on the kitchen floor in front of a box fan. My mother gave me a cold glass of water. I could tell she was worried about me. I was sunburned all over my body, and my speech was slurred because of exhaustion. I said to her, "Do you think he will be proud of me this time, Mama?" She replied, "Yes, baby, he will. But let me tell you this. If he isn't or if he screams at you, I promise you: We are leaving this house and never coming back!"

It was like a TV drama. Just seconds after her statement, my father walked in the door. I pulled myself up from the floor when he came in the kitchen. I said to him, "Daddy, did you see that I cut all the grass? I did it all by myself!" His reply cut me deeper than he could have ever imagined.

It was not so much what he said. It was all the years of hurt that had built towards that moment. My spirit was weak and beaten down. I was a kid. I didn't understand why my life was the way it was. All I wanted to do was make my father proud.

All I wanted to do was make
my father proud.

He looked at me and said, "Yeah, I saw it. I saw that you didn't finish it. You never finish anything you start. Now, get up and get back out there and finish the job. I don't care how tired you are. Can you just do what I tell you to do?" Then he walked out.

I realize this doesn't seem like a huge, life-altering moment. How could a father, pointing out that his son had missed an area of grass to cut, change the life of that boy?

It wasn't that day alone. It was a culmination of all the days just like that. Years full of physical, mental, and verbal abuse had built up inside my mother. This day was the tipping point. It was the last straw. She had finally had enough.

My mother looked at me, "That's it. We are gone. It's over, son." We left that day. I thought my pain was over. I didn't realize it had just begun.

Chapter Three

Be Careful What You Ask For

The Flight of the Green Machine

The "Green Machine" was what we called our green Chrysler station wagon. It had been in the family for years. Yes, it was green. And to help your mental picture of this moment even more, it had fake brown wooden panels on every door. These were very popular in the 1970s and '80s.

On this day, the Green Machine would play a different role.

Many times, we had thrown our belongings in the old faithful family chariot and attempted to get away from the pain and hurt of our home. Every time, we would get a couple of miles down the road, only to be met by my father. He would beg my mother to forgive him. He would promise the moon, and my mother would always agree to give him "just one more chance." We would turn old "Green" back around and head back home. In my heart, I would always hope that my father meant what he said.

This time was different. Mama just kept driving. Honestly, I don't remember where we stayed that night. It was all a blur for me. I was a kid, a confused and messed-up kid. My heart was torn. I was so happy to finally leave, but I also desperately wanted my family to stay together. Truthfully, there was little doubt in my mind that we would probably end up back at home, going through it all over again.

But we didn't go back. We never went back to my father.

That day, my mother began the life of a "single parent." She would remain a single mother for the rest of my childhood and into my adult life. She didn't know what to do next. I certainly didn't know what to do next. The only thing we knew was that we were together. I knew my mother loved me and my younger brother, and she would fight for us, no matter what.

Trying to Drown a Destiny

Most of us know the story of Moses. He is known all over the world as the "deliverer" of the people of God from the bondage of Pharaoh in Egypt. But his story did not begin with the famous words, "Pharaoh, let my people go."

The Word tells us: "And Joseph died, all his brothers, and all that generation. But the children of Israel were fruitful and increased abundantly, multiplied and grew exceedingly mighty; and the land was filled with them. Now there arose a new king over Egypt, who did not know Joseph. And he said to his people, 'Look, the people of the children of Israel are more and mightier than we; come, let us deal shrewdly with them, lest they multiply, and it happen, in the event of war, that they also join our enemies and fight against us, and so go up out of the land'" (Exodus 1:6–10).

Egypt had prospered greatly because of the kind treatment they had offered the people of Israel on behalf of Joseph. But after the death of Joseph, things changed dramatically. Out of fear, the new Pharaoh made the people of God into slaves.

But that wasn't enough. He realized that if he was going to stop them from growing larger in number than the Egyptians, he had to stop the seed of the people of God. Pharaoh had to eliminate the men from ever becoming all they were supposed to be. So, under the influence of Satan, he struck at the very heart of the culture of God's people—the family structure.

He called the Egyptian midwives to his palace and gave them instructions. "Then the king of Egypt spoke to the Hebrew midwives … and he said, 'When you do the duties of a midwife for the Hebrew women, and see them on the birthstools, if it is a son, then you shall kill him; but if it is a daughter, then she shall live.' But the midwives feared God, and did not do as the king of Egypt commanded them, but saved the male children alive" (Exodus 1:15–17).

The midwives were not crazy. They had seen the favor of God on the descendants of Joseph. They had grown to love them, so they refused to kill the boys. Pharaoh found out about the rebellion of the midwives and spoke yet another decree in anger. "Then Pharaoh gave this order to all his people: 'Every Hebrew boy that is born you must throw into the Nile, but let every girl live'" (Exodus 1:22 NIV).

Every action of Pharaoh was directed by the Enemy of God – Satan. The Devil knew that if he could kill these boys when they were babies, he would kill their destiny. It has always been the plan of our adversary to kill children before they can find out who they are in God. He doesn't care if he kills their destiny through actually taking their lives or through causing their lives to be so abusive, dysfunctional, and painful that they never recover. Either way works for him.

Most of "who we are," on every level, was shaped in our childhood. Adults from all walks of life are still dealing with things that happened to them, and around them, as children. Addictions, suicidal thoughts, lack of self-worth, low motivation, reckless behavior, and many other "adult issues" can be traced to our childhood.

Adults from all walks of life are still dealing with things that happened to them, and around them, as children.

Pharaoh wanted to "kill" all boys out of fear, but Satan wanted Moses dead.

Something Is Hidden

Most of us have heard the old corny joke: "Without my mother, I truly wouldn't be here." This is, of course, true of all of us. Regardless of whether we know our mothers or not, we all had a mother. Without his mother, Moses could have never become the man he was. Without his mother, he could have never walked in his destiny.

The same is true of me. I would not be sitting in a hotel room writing a book about my life, or walking in the plan of God for my life, if it were not for my mother. The night she finally left my father saved my life.

I am not saying that I felt like my father would have taken my life. I believe he really loved me (in his own way). I am simply saying that it began a process of finding myself that would have never happened without the sequence of events that was unfolding right before my young eyes.

After a few days of staying with family, we eventually found our home. My mother found us an apartment in the "housing projects" of a small town not far from my former home. It was a nice place, but it felt very strange to no longer live in our old house. It smelled like it had just been cleaned with industrial-strength bleach. I think it stayed that way the entire time we were living there. We quickly made friends with some of our neighbors and began to assimilate into our new environment.

We were there because my mother had found a safe place for my brother and me. No one did it for her; she did it herself. She quickly became a fiercely independent woman. I look back on it now, and I see the power of God on her life. He enabled her to do things that she was not naturally equipped or educated to do.

Little did I know, my mother was tormented inside. My mother had a secret.

She seemed happy for the first time in years. We didn't have much, but we felt free. I saw her laughing for the first time in a long time. Even though I was still just a boy, I saw the change in her for the better. Little did I know, my mother was tormented inside. My mother had a secret. I would soon find it out, and it would change my life forever.

Hidden Secrets Can't Last Forever

After the decree of Pharaoh that all baby Hebrew boys were to be thrown in the river to die, Moses' mother made a decision to hide her son from danger.

"So the woman conceived and bore a son. And when she saw that he was a beautiful child, she hid him three months. But when she could no longer hide him, she took an ark of bulrushes for him, daubed it with asphalt and pitch, put the child in it, and laid it in the reeds by the river's bank" (Exodus 2:2–3).

Mama made a "mama" decision. She chose to put her life in danger for the sake of her child.

Who would have ever imagined such a plan?

After three months, she realized that it was impossible to "hide" him any longer. So she made a boat out of weeds and put him in it. She put this makeshift ark in the Nile River, and gently pushed him away. Her total faith was in God at that point. She didn't know what she was doing. She didn't know if she would ever see her son again, but her mother's instinct was to save her son.

I love to break down the non-famous characters of Scripture. Moses is the star of the story to the masses, but his mother is the hero of the Big Picture. Without her decision to do everything she could to protect her son, who knows how the story would have gone?

The river that her own father had decreed would be the death of Moses ended up being the very thing that saved his life.

Pharaoh's daughter just "happened" to be coming down into the river to bathe, and she spotted the small boat with the little baby Hebrew boy inside. The Bible says that she had "compassion" for the child (see Exodus 2:6). One of her royal entourage was instructed to "draw out" the boy and bring him to her. At that moment, she decided to take him as her own son. "So she called his name Moses, saying, 'Because I drew him out of the water'" (Exodus 2:10).

The river that her own father had decreed would be the death of Moses ended up being the very thing that saved his life and set into motion a destiny that would change the world!

A Little Drummer Boy

I was your typical boy of the late 1970s and early 1980s. I loved video games, but I had also loved playing army and building forts in the woods next to my childhood home. Summers on our hillside meant my cousins and I would leave the house early and head out to our adventures, only to return shortly before supper or bedtime.

Many times, I rode my bicycle for miles just to see my friends and hang out. I have many memories of me and my best friend just riding, pretending that we were on motorcycles traveling the world. My bike was my transportation. It was also my getaway.

Things changed dramatically after the move. I no longer had our family "woods" to fight against imaginary enemies. I couldn't play with my cousins on our hillside. I was living in a town where I knew no one except my mother and my brother.

One day, I decided to ride my bike all over my new small town. I rode it up to Main Street and back down many of the side roads. It was very different from my home, where we only had one road in and one road out. After riding for a couple of hours, I made it back to the projects. But something wouldn't let me pull into our community just yet.

Right across the street from our complex was a church. We had visited a couple of times. I didn't really know anything about it, except that it had the same name as the church I had been raised in. What I mean is that it had the same denominational name on the sign. I was too young to even know what a denomination was.

That day I felt compelled to just ride over to that church. I remember circling in the parking lot many times. Then as if I had just been translated there, I found myself suddenly pulling into the driveway of the church parsonage. Before I knew it, I was knocking on the door. I can't explain it. I wasn't nervous. I just knocked on the door.

The pastor of the church slowly opened the door, and said, "Can I help you, son?" Without hesitation, I said "My name is Larry. I live across the street. I was just wondering if you need a drummer to play in your church?" His reply was quick and decisive, "I've been praying for God to send us a drummer."

I was by no means a professional percussionist. In fact, I mostly just played the snare and the high-hat cymbal. But I could keep a beat. Not long after that bike ride, the pastor bought a new drum set and told the church I was the new drummer.

My life was great. I was starting to make new friends. I was no longer in an abusive situation, and now I was "living the teenage rock star dream." I would soon find out that my idea of where my life was headed was about to take an unexpected turn.

A Sheltered Life

Moses was raised by Egyptian parents. He was raised in an Egyptian culture. Everything he knew was Egyptian, but something never seemed right about the situation.

One of the most remarkable parts of his story happened when his mother placed him in the river. God used that moment to make a way for his birth mother to actually raise him and nurture him.

The Bible says that when Pharaoh's daughter drew Moses out of the water, his sister Miriam was watching close by. Miriam sensed a perfect opportunity and said, "'Shall I go and call a nurse for you from the Hebrew women, that she may nurse the child for you?' And Pharaoh's daughter said to her, 'Go.' So the maiden went and called the child's mother. Then Pharaoh's daughter said to her, 'Take this child away and nurse him for me, and I will give you your wages.' So the woman took the child and nursed him. And the child grew, and she brought him to Pharaoh's daughter, and he became her son" (Exodus 2:7–10).

Take a moment to let this miraculous moment sink in. Moses' mother did everything she could to protect him, but she had to just let him go and give him to God. When she could no longer hide the truth and released him, God saved him and gave him back to her!

The Lord honored this mother's heart and, through a miraculous turn of events, caused her to actually get to raise her child and even nurse him. Wow! On top of everything else, she was paid to protect and feed her own son!

His mother fed him, but she also taught him. For years, Egypt trained him with the best scholars in the world. He must have been one of the most intelligent young men to ever live in Egypt. But secretly, his mother prayed that he would never lose his connection to his true people. She ensured he stayed alive, but she also ensured he would be ready when his moment came.

His life was sheltered. He did not suffer with his people, but in his heart, there was some kind of connection that he couldn't explain. He knew there was more to the story than what he had been told. He knew there were secrets. His mother had told him some things, but He didn't know everything about his past. He certainly didn't know what was about to happen to shape his future. The sheltered life was about to be shattered!

Shot to the Heart

It was like any other day. It was summer and it was hot. We had air conditioning, but we were not running it all the time. We had to save on the electricity bill. Of course, living in the South, we had a screen door. The regular door was open, but the screen door was closed. It kept the bugs out, but you could hear everything outside.

I heard a vehicle pull up in front of our home. I quickly realized it was my father. He got out of the truck, yelling for my mother. All the feelings of fear that had gripped me most of my life instantly flushed through my nervous system. It was as if all the weeks of joy and freedom were gone. I knew this drill. I knew what was about to go down!

Sure enough, my father came in the house, and said he wanted to talk to my mother and to me. My little brother was there, too, but he was in the next room playing. I know he was aware that something was going on, but he was not old enough to really grasp the moment.

The picture of that moment is still very clear in my mind's eye today. I remember my father sitting down at the kitchen table and begging my mother to come home. He seemed really broken. I believe that in his heart, he just didn't know what to do with his life.

I am sure, in all his troubles with my mother, he never envisioned his life alone. He knew it was bad, but he still thought he could talk her in to coming back.

But shortly into the conversation, it became apparent that this was not like all the other times. He could see something different in my mother's eyes. She was not buying it, and she was not giving in. I saw a strength in her that day. She had been beaten down physically and mentally in the past, but not today. She said, "I am not coming back today or ever. It is time you understand that."

The atmosphere changed dramatically. I was standing in the kitchen next to the refrigerator. I had not said much during the whole conversation. My father turned and looked at me and said, "Tell your mother to come home. I know you want to come home." My heart felt like it was going to explode. I was shaking, but I mustered as much boldness as I could and said, "No, Daddy. We are not coming home."

My mother was not the only one who had something different in her eyes that day. My father could see that something had changed in me, too. There was a boldness in me that had replaced the paralyzing fear I had shown before. Going to the church across the street and playing the drums had given me a sense of purpose. Even though I was a kid, I felt a sense of belonging. I knew I was supposed to be right where I was.

"What did you say, boy?" he shouted. I said again, "Mama said we are not coming back, so we are not coming back." He just stopped talking for a few seconds. I didn't realize it at the time, but he was thinking about what he was about to do.

He pulled out a pistol of some kind and laid it on the kitchen table in front of him. He looked me straight in the eye, and made sure I knew it was loaded. He cocked the pistol and placed it to the temple of his head. He was shaking. I think he was really scared. You could see the scenarios playing through his head. It was extremely tense and quiet.

Then the silence broke when he said, "Larry, look at me. I want you to know that when I leave this place today, it will be the last time you ever see me. You could have stopped this. You could make your mother come home, but you won't do it. I am leaving here, and I'm driving up the road. I am going to park my truck, and I am going to blow my brains out. You will have to live with that the rest of your life. Is that what you want?"

I cried out, "Daddy, don't do it. Please don't do it." He got up and stormed out. I heard him say as he walked across the short piece of grass we called our yard, "Remember what I said." He got in his truck and sped off.

I collapsed on the floor of the kitchen. I was destroyed once again.

It All Makes Sense Now

Moses had lived in luxury while the Hebrew people were suffering in slavery. He was raised to believe he was Egyptian, but it was all a lie. He couldn't understand why his heart would race whenever he saw the children of Israel suffer. He was covered in gold and precious stones, but it couldn't cover his inner turmoil.

His mother had secretly dropped hints; and at other times, spoken openly to him about his heritage. But she was careful not to tell him "everything," so he would not put his life in jeopardy. He lived forty years in the palace. He was known throughout all the land, as the grandson of Pharaoh.

One day he witnessed an Egyptian man beating a Hebrew man. He had seen this treatment hundreds of times before. But there was something different about this day.

I can only imagine the internal struggle going on inside of him. Not only was his physical DNA connected to the Hebrew people, but his spirit man was screaming at him to stand up and make a difference. He knew this was not right, but what could he do?

Without a second thought, he looked all around to make sure no one was looking and then jumped into the fight. He grabbed the Egyptian man, threw him to the ground, and killed him. Then he buried the body. No one saw him, so he got away with it. He could go on with his life as normal.

Not long after that, he saw two Hebrew men fighting and said to them, "Why are you fighting your brother?" He was shocked to hear one of them reply, "Why are you judging us? Are you going to kill us like you killed the Egyptian?" (Exodus 2:11–14, author's paraphrase).

Moses immediately feared for his life. He knew Pharaoh would kill him if he found out someone from his own household had killed a fellow Egyptian. He dropped everything and ran.

When he woke up that day, it had been like any other day, or so he thought. But it was not like any other day. It was the day Moses was to find out who he really was.

When he was running for his life, he realized for the first time why his heart never felt at home in Pharaoh's palace. He had lost his identity but had finally found peace. With each step taking him further away from all that he had ever known, he grew closer and closer to the truth. He was running for his life, but he had never felt more alive.

I can almost see him stopping to rest under a shade tree. He was all alone. His mother was not there. His sister was not there. His adoptive Egyptian mother was not there. He was cold, and he was alone. But I can hear him say, "It all makes sense now."

Two Words

As my father raced his truck down our driveway, I lay on the kitchen floor. All the memories and pain of my life were back. I felt complete hopelessness. I was stuck. It felt like I was the only person in the world that had to deal with this. It seemed like all my friends' families were perfect. (Of course, I later found out that many of them were just as dysfunctional as mine. Nothing is ever really what it seems.)

I think I must say something important regarding my father.

I don't think he was aware of the damage he was doing. I don't think he realized that he was systematically taking me apart, piece by piece. I don't think he knew how damaging his words and actions were to my life. In fact, later in my life, I found out that his father had treated him in basically the same way when he was a child. There is no excuse for this type of behavior, but I do know that many times people raise their kids exactly the way they were raised. This is referred to as generational curses or duplication. Nevertheless, whether he knew it or not, that day was the most devastating day of my short life.

My mother pulled me off the floor and took me to the couch. I was crying, sobbing. She was crying. My brother was crying. We were all crying. My cries became louder and I became angry. I started saying, "Why does it have to be this way? Why does he have to be this way? Do you think he's really going to kill himself? It's all my fault! If he does it, it is my fault."

Mama was becoming hysterical. She was watching me intently; it was killing her to not be able to help me. She could see I was losing it. I may have been on the verge of a nervous breakdown. Something was going to have to give. Something was about to break. I remember quickly replaying all the words he said again in my mind. The more I thought about them, the more my idea of that moment began to change.

Rather quickly, my hurt and pain turned to rage. I became angry and started screaming, "I hate that man. I hate him. I don't ever want to see him again." Even though that was not true, I meant it at that moment. I continued to scream, "I hate him, I hate him, I hate him."

Then I said something I am sure I had thought a hundred times in my head, but never said out loud. I screamed at the top of my lungs: "I WISH HE WASN'T MY FATHER!" There was about three seconds of silence, and then I heard two words from my mother. Two words that shook me to the core. Two words I never once imagined I would hear her say.

She said, "He's not."

True Identity

Moses fled for his life. He ended up in a desert. He went from a sumptuous palace to a very dry place. He went from having hundreds of people take care of his every need to being completely alone. He was tired, scared, and very thirsty.

Exodus 2:15 says Moses "sat down by a well." This was not just any well. It would be the place where he would find his wife and companion for life.

He knew he would be thirsty. He knew that thirst would bring him to the place where he would meet the love of his life.

You need to get this in your spirit. God knew everything that would happen in Moses' life. He knew he would need to be protected as a young man from the truth of his real identity. He knew the time would come in which a horrible situation would cause him to rise up and search for the truth. He knew that when he learned the truth, he would run. He knew he would be thirsty. He knew that thirst would bring him to the place where he would meet the love of his life. He knew the desert experience would mold him into the man he would need to be when it was time to go back and face Pharaoh and set his people free.

That well represented the hand of God in his life. The Lord brought water to him in the desert. Moses needed to know that God was on his side and would provide for him.

Later in his life, he would see God supernaturally provide water on a couple of occasions for millions of people. Moses had this "well experience" so that he could teach the people in the desert later. He could tell them, "At my lowest point, God changed my life at a well." It was all a part of the preparation of what was to come.

Superhero Dad

"He's not." Those two words sent shock waves throughout my whole spirit, soul, and body. I replied to my mother, "What did you say?" She said again, "He's not your father. I've been wanting to tell you this your whole life. I know this is a shock, but it's time you know the truth."

While my younger brother played in the next room, my mother began to tell me of an almost mythical man who showed her love when she had only received abuse. She said, "I wasn't looking for this, Larry, you have to know that. I was broken, and didn't feel like I would ever be loved. He loved me and respected me."

I could tell that it felt like a thousand pounds had been lifted off her. She could tell my little mind was spinning with this new life-changing revelation, but it was almost as if she knew that this was the moment to tell me everything.

After a couple of hours of talking, I learned of a man that seemed larger than life. This man—who was my father—was an incredible man. He had fought to keep me. He had begged my mom to leave so we could be together. He had loved me from birth. It was a dream.

At that moment, I set a goal in my life. I would find this man somehow. One day I would have a dream relationship with my father. He was out there. He was probably thinking about me right at that moment. He was dreaming of the day we would begin our lifelong relationship as father and son.

Did I have other brothers and sisters? Are they older or younger than me? Where did my father live? What did he look like? Did I look just like him? My mother said I looked just like him! Wow!

She told me he was a hunter and a fisherman, and that he loved sports. He was also a professional chef and many other things. He was truly Super Dad. He was everything a boy could ever ask for.

There was only one problem. We had no idea where he was or how to even find him. My mother had not heard from him since I was about three years old.

Pain That Births Clarity

God knows everything that is going to happen in our lives. He is intimately involved in every aspect of our existence. Nothing catches Him by surprise. He truly cares about every detail, every pain, and every offense.

The Lord knew the truth about me, even though I didn't. He knew, regardless of the hurt from my father, that the truth would be extremely difficult to hear. God knew it would come out in the midst of being wounded. God knew my pain would give birth to clarity.

God knew my pain would give birth to clarity.

Now it all made sense on many levels. I never really looked like my father. I always wondered why my friends looked like their dads, and I didn't resemble mine. I had blond hair, and my father had jet-black hair.

Even though I don't think he hated me, it truly seemed as if he did. I would wonder, "What is it about me that causes such rage toward me?" He probably knew the truth about me. When he looked at me, he didn't see his son. He saw another man's son, and he couldn't handle that. So he took his pain and hurt out on me.

There is never an excuse for the abuse—physical, verbal or emotional—of another human being. My father needed a "well experience."

God is leading all of us to just "sit down by the well." But we are the ones who have to be prepared to accept it. At that moment in his life, my dad was not prepared to sit down and drink from the well.

My father did not kill himself that day. We would go on to weather many more fights as I grew older. It would take years before I ever heard him say, "You're not my son." But that day did come, many years later.

Burning Bush Experience

Moses was forty years old when he fled Egypt. He found his wife in the deserts of Midian and became a shepherd. He lived the simple life of a shepherd for another forty years. But one day, that all changed.

Moses was leading his flock around the mountain of Horeb as he had done hundreds of times before. But today was different.

There was a small tree (or bush) along the path. I am sure Moses had passed it many times. He probably sat under its shade a few times to rest. He wasn't thinking about that tree. There was really nothing special about it in the eyes.

But one "seemingly random day," the bush seemed to be on fire. Exodus 3 tells the story of this day.

The bush was on fire, but not being consumed by the flames. Moses had never seen anything like this, so he turned to take a closer look. At that moment, he heard God speak from the bush. God told Moses that the place where he was standing was holy ground.

Everyone has their own "burning bush" experience at some point in their life.

God said, "Moses, I have heard the cry of My people. I'm going to send you back to Egypt and you are going to tell Pharaoh to release My people and let them go free" (Exodus 3:1–10, author's paraphrase). Moses thought God had missed it and had the wrong person!

After a lot of debate with God, Moses agreed—and the rest is history! Spoiler alert! After ten plagues, Moses led them out of Egypt and to their freedom.

Everyone has their own "burning bush" experience at some point in their life. You just know that this has to be God. It would be impossible any other way. The bush was on fire, but it was not consumed. It was supernatural.

I was about to have one of those supernatural moments in my life. No, I didn't see a literal bush on fire, but I experienced something so supernatural and amazing that it is still hard for me to believe it actually happened.

That Was Weird

My mother told me about my biological father when I was in fifth grade. I kept it a secret from that point forward. The legend of this man only grew larger and larger in my heart over the years to come. I had still never even seen a picture of him, but he was a giant to me.

It is very difficult to keep something like this a secret for five years. It's hard to keep anything a secret that long. Can you imagine a teenager keeping a secret this extraordinary? But somehow, I did. I kept it from everyone.

After a season of legal battles between my parents, we were eventually awarded our old home. My father was told he would have to find another place to live. I was very happy to be back in my "old stomping grounds." Unfortunately, that meant we were disconnected from the church in which I was playing drums. As I got older, I simply got out of church altogether.

Fast forward to tenth grade. It was a day like every other day. Nothing special at all.

I was in typing class (yes, that was a thing back then). We had finished our assignment, and I was hanging out over in the corner with some of my friends. Something was said that, apparently, I thought was funny. I laughed really loud.

Just then, one of my friends looked at me and said, "That was weird." I said, "What was weird?" She replied, "You just looked so much like someone I know!" I brushed it off, and said something like, "OK, whatever."

It happened several times again, and it was beginning to bother me a little. I finally said one day, "Who do you keep saying I look like?" She said, "I know it's weird, but you look like my stepfather."

Just for fun, I said, "What's his name?" Her answer caused me to shudder. She told me his name, and it was the first name of my real father. Then she told me his last name. It was also the same as my father's.

In my heart, I told myself this was nothing. There was no way it could be him. Just to settle my mind and move on, I asked her if she knew his birthday. She said, "Yes, it is ——." I almost threw up. It was the same as my father's birthday.

I excused myself from the room and went into the bathroom; I had to get myself together. Could I have just located my real father by simply laughing in a typing class? Could this really be happening?

When I got home, I told my mother everything that transpired. She was in shock and asked me, "Did she say where he is living?" I told her, "Yes, he is supposed to be living in the city of ——." My mom screamed out, "Are you kidding? That's where he has always lived. I can't believe he is still there!"

Hello?

I vividly remember sitting in the movie theater with my brother and hearing the famous words spoken to Luke: "I am your father!" We both (along with the whole theater) yelled in shock, "No!" That scene would become real to me on another level the day I told my mother what had happened in typing class.

She asked me, "Do you want to call the operator and try to find his number and call him?" Without hesitation, I said, "Yes, I want to know the truth if this is him." The operator said there were three that matched his name in that city.

I dialed the first one. I heard the phone ringing in my ears. I believe it rang three times. Then I heard a deep voice say, "Hello." I had been so brave just seconds earlier. But at that moment I froze. I couldn't say a word. Again, I heard, "Hello," and again I said nothing.

Then I heard words that were only a dream just moments earlier. "Larry, is that you? I've been waiting for years for this moment. Is that you?" I was stunned, but I mustered up the strength to speak. I replied to him, "I'm going to ask you one question, and then I am hanging the phone up. All I want to know is… Are you my father?"

"I am your father, and I love you." Click. I hung up the phone and looked at my mother and said, "It's really him."

Chapter Four

Lessons from a Redwood King

Father and Son

I hung up the phone that night, looked at my mother, and said, "It's him." I really had no idea how quickly things would escalate after that phone call.

I had never seen my real father. I had no idea what he looked like. But make no mistake about it, I had created an image of him in my mind. I envisioned him as a "man's man" who was also loving and wanted to spend all of his spare time with his son. I actually had dreams of him sitting around thinking about me, and wanting to be in my life. I didn't know him, but I knew once I was with him, he would teach me everything I needed to know to be a good man.

Within just a few days, conversations began between my mother and my biological father. I was told that he wanted to see me. I was excited, but also scared to death. Would he be everything I dreamed, or would my hopes be dashed? Would I look like him? Did we have anything in common?

I had no time to think about it. Before I could even process what was happening, I was in the Green Machine headed to meet him. It was only about an hour and a half from my home. Can you imagine? All these years, my real father had lived less than two hours away from me.

As our car came to a stop, I noticed a pickup truck waiting at the spot. I froze. The moment I had dreamed of since fifth grade was coming true. I had rehearsed how I was going to act, and what I would say in that moment. But for some reason, I couldn't move. I just sat and looked at his truck.

Then, like in a movie, the driver's side door slowly opened and a giant of a man stepped out. He was about six foot four, but in my mind he looked like he was seven feet tall. I'm not kidding when I say it felt like he was walking in slow motion and a powerful rock ballad was playing in the background behind him!

It was better than a dream. It was real life, and he was everything I had expected and more. I got out of the car and walked up to him. He smiled and said, "Hello, Larry, I am so happy to see you."

I looked at his face, and I realized I looked just like him. He was much taller than me, but there was absolutely no denying I was his son. My eyes, nose, chin, and even the way I talked was like him. I later realized we even laughed the same way. After a brief, awkward moment, it got even more awkward. I got in his truck and went to spend the night in his home.

Think about this: just weeks earlier, my laugh and expressions had reminded my friend of her stepfather. That stepfather turned out to be my father. Now I was spending the night in his house. It was surreal, to say the least.

Positioned for Greatness

Most people have heard the story of David. He is the shepherd boy who would become Israel's greatest king. His journey from the deserts to the palace is one of true legend.

We all know of his famous victory against Goliath. This giant came out every day and mocked the people of God. He challenged the armies of Israel to fight him, but no one dared to stand against this warrior.

Jesse, David's father, had sent David to the battlefield with food for his brothers. As he arrived, he could hear Goliath shouting and cursing from the mountaintop. Without hesitation, David exclaimed, "Who is this Philistine, defying the armies of God?" Instead of fighting, his brothers and their fellow soldiers ran and hid in fear. While everyone else was making excuses and giving reasons why it didn't make sense to challenge Goliath, David asked a pointed question: "Is there not a cause?" (1 Samuel 17:29b).

He realized that he hadn't set out looking for a fight that day, but the fight had found him. David understood honor. He was not going to allow this heathen barbarian to mock God's people and their king.

Honor was at the core of David's being. He wouldn't dare fight Goliath without the permission and blessing of the king. He honored King Saul.

After speaking with the king, he politely turned down King Saul's offer to wear his personal armor in the battle. David simply replied, "Thank you, but I think I will just take my sling."

Then it happened. With one smooth stone, he took down a man that had struck fear in the hearts of the entire army of Israel. David brought the head of the giant back and placed it at the feet of Saul.

This battle was fought to honor God, but it was also to honor the king. This act of integrity would set the stage for David's coming reign as king himself.

This battle was fought to honor God, but it was also to honor the king.

David loved his father, Jesse, but he realized that he also needed to serve another father in his life—King Saul. He would soon be a personal assistant to the king. He played music for him and made sure he was taken care of. He was King Saul's armor-bearer.

He eventually married the king's daughter. Matrimony into the kingdom made David a son of Saul. He thought he was living the dream!

Whirlwind

Within just a few days of hearing the voice of my real father for the first time, he and my mother were talking. I don't know what all they talked about, but it was obviously very emotional for the both of them.

It was also quickly noticeable that the connection between them still existed. It was not only because of me, either; they had truly been in love. Not long after that first conversation, he separated from his current wife and began to pursue my mother.

Once my mom knew she could talk about my real father to me, she began to tell me many stories of their brief time together. She explained how he had been such a gentleman to her; he had loved her and showed her respect like no man had ever before, or since.

Every story was prefaced with an apology and a statement of embarrassment. She would say things like, "Larry, I am sorry about all of this. I am ashamed of what I did, but I am not ashamed of you." She had lived with the guilt of having an affair for my entire life. She never regretted what came out of the relationship—me—but she had lived in a self-imposed prison of shame because of the act itself.

I remember telling her, "Mama, no one blames you for desiring to be loved and respected. I want you to be happy. You deserve it after all you've been through."

I knew adultery is sin, and my mama knew it, too. She had long ago repented to God for that. He had forgiven her, but she had not forgiven herself. I encouraged her that it was time to let it go and move forward. Move forward is exactly what they did.

At breakneck speed, they quickly picked up where they had left off shortly after my birth. My biological mother and father were dating and falling in love again. It felt like all my dreams were coming true.

My biological mother and father were dating and falling in love again. It felt like all my dreams were coming true.

Not only were they hitting it off, but he and I were living the "father and son life." He took me all over his hometown and showed me off to everyone we met. He never held back in letting them know who I was. "I want you to meet my son. This is Larry. He's come back into my life and it is just great."

I couldn't believe how easy it was for him to tell people about me. It didn't stop there. He took me to his job and let me help him at work. We went fishing and did outdoor activities together. He gave me gifts. It was incredible. I felt like I had known him all my life.

The Assumed Life

Because of the miraculous victory over Goliath, David quickly became a legend in the house of Israel. The women in the streets sang a song: "Saul has killed thousands, but David has killed tens of thousands!" (See 1 Samuel 18:7.) David honored the house of Saul and never expected royal treatment. But he was now married into the family and on the "inside." He became very close friends with King Saul's son, Jonathan. They fought in battles together and got to know each other well. Everything David did was to honor Saul. But Saul didn't return the favor.

He was extremely jealous of David and eventually set out a plan to kill him. When Jonathan heard of the plot to take David's life, he made sure he told him of the plan. Jonathan devised a strategy for David to escape and run for his life. That is exactly what he did.

When Saul found out about it, he was enraged. He quickly summoned his best forces and pursued David. He commanded his troops to "shoot to kill." He chased David all over the land of Israel. Each time, David somehow avoided death or capture.

Through it all, David never stopped wanting to restore his relationship with Saul. He never stopped honoring the house of his king. Many of David's followers often encouraged him to fight Saul and take the kingdom for himself. But he wouldn't do it.

David had a right to the kingdom. The prophet Samuel had already anointed him king, even while he was still just a shepherd (see 1 Samuel 16:1–13).

Saul just assumed his son Jonathan would be the next king. This is the protocol of a kingdom. In the royal lineage of the monarchy, Jonathan's son would be king after him and so on. The name of Jonathan's son was Mephibosheth. He was royalty, too.

Mephibosheth had the dream life. His father loved him. His grandfather loved him. There was an entire group of women assigned to take care of the future king. He was only five years old when the Bible introduces us to this young prince.

It seemed as if it was all laid out perfectly for him. That is, until a fateful day that would make Mephibosheth a household name.

The Trip of a Lifetime

It seemed like an eternity, but it had only been a few months since my miraculous discovery of my biological father. Everything in my life was now secondary to my father. I played football and had several other activities going on in school, but I didn't care about any of them. Something amazing had happened in my life, and I now had a shot to learn what it took to be a man.

As if all the other stuff going on was not enough to make me feel like I was dreaming, my mother shocked me with more exciting news. "We are going on a trip across America with your father. He bought a travel trailer, and we are going to drive to the California coast. We are going to see the country together as a family!"

What? Pinch me! I was going to get to see things only a few people will ever be blessed to see. And the icing on the cake was: I would have this time to get to know my father better.

We bought a map and traced our route with a marker. Then we laid out our planned stops, and how long we would get to stay to see each place. It was exciting drawing a line across this great country, and realizing you were going to get to see all of it.

We set out in an early '80s Suburban, pulling a sixteen-foot camper. I don't really think I grasped that we were about to drive thousands of miles in two weeks. Many of the places we saw were through the window at fifty-five miles per hour! But we did get to see some amazing things along the journey.

Hundreds of pictures were taken of the scenery and of our new family together. I made sure several were taken of me and my father!

Mississippi, Louisiana, Texas, New Mexico, Colorado, Wyoming, Utah, Arizona, Nevada, California, Oregon. The Grand Canyon, Yellowstone, Las Vegas, Los Angeles. We saw all sorts of odd and strange monuments on the road to the West Coast. But for me, they all paled in comparison to one of the final destinations: the Redwood Forest.

Rooted and Connected

If you would permit me, I would like to take a brief side trail from my story. I need to talk about these great trees.

I don't really know how to even describe these giants. You can watch videos or look at pictures of these magnificent creations, but you will never fully grasp their majesty until you stand at the base of one.

These trees made such a mark on my life that I have preached entire series about them. I have told my wife and kids about them many times. Unfortunately, I have not been able to take my family to see them. Taking them there is on the proverbial "bucket list."

The redwoods teach us so much about the kingdom of God. In creation, they are the epitome of greatness, but there is so much more to them than what you see. They are a miracle of God.

The redwoods teach us so much about the kingdom of God. In creation, they are the epitome of greatness.

The tallest of all the redwoods is a staggering three hundred and seventy feet. That is seventy feet higher than a football field is long! Many others stand two hundred and fifty to three hundred feet tall. Experts believe several of the ones that were cut down had reached 400+ feet!

The way redwoods are sustained with water and nutrients is nothing short of miraculous. The only way humans can bring water from ground level to that height is by using multiple mechanical pumps.

Redwoods maintain a constant upward flow of water from the roots to the top of the tree. It is believed that the water molecules interact with the capillary tubes of the trees to create a system that "drags" the water up the tree. This suction is impacted even more by the water evaporating through the leaves at the tops of the trees. As the water evaporates, it creates an even greater suction. But as great as that is, it is not enough. The redwoods make up the difference needed by *creating their own rain*. The trees use the fog that rolls in daily from the West Coast and convert it to rain.

The most powerful thing I learned was the key to their survival and longevity. They have survived every natural disaster and weather event for over two thousand years. What is the key to their staying power and growth? Their roots.

Just as a skyscraper needs a very deep foundation to support the weight of the building, you would think these giants would need very deep roots as well. Not so. A redwood that stands three hundred feet high has roots that are only six to eight feet deep! That's amazing!

You would think a tree that was so top-heavy would never be able to survive a strong wind. Even though their roots are shallow, they stretch outwards hundreds of feet! This gives the trees greater stability.

God is a relational God. He uses nature to teach us spiritual principles. As each individual redwood tree's roots go wide, they begin to intertwine with other redwood tree's roots. They actually "fuse" together and, in essence, built one giant root ball the size of the whole forest!

David lived in the F.O.G. (Favor of God), so he stayed in the rain of God's presence.

One tree can't come down, because all the other trees are holding it up!

The Redwood King

King David was a human redwood. He refused to allow himself to "grow higher" without connecting and honoring those who were in the forest with him. He was not going to "cut" himself away from those he should honor. He understood that when a person messed up, it didn't disqualify him for future service. David believed in the power of restoration! He was a rooted man. He was a man after God's own heart.

David lived in the F.O.G. (Favor of God), so he stayed in the rain of God's presence. Just like the mighty redwoods use the fog to make their own rain, David stayed in the F.O.G. to keep himself alive.

On one occasion, David was given the perfect opportunity to "cut" down the mighty tree of the kingdom of Saul. The armies of the king were pursuing David and suddenly decided to stop by a cave. They were there "to take care of business." Saul also went into the cave. He had no idea that David and his men were camping in the back of the cave and could see them.

"Then the men of David said to him, 'This is the day of which the Lord said to you, "Behold, I will deliver your enemy into your hand, that you may do to him as it seems good to you"'" (1 Samuel 24:4).

David quickly rebuked them and replied, "'The Lord forbid that I should do this thing to my master, the Lord's anointed, to stretch out my hand against him, seeing he is the anointed of the Lord.' So David restrained his servants with these words, and did not allow them to rise against Saul. And Saul got up from the cave and went on his way" (1 Samuel 24:6–7).

David's loyalty would not stop with Saul. We will see later that it extended to Saul's entire family, and to a young man named Mephibosheth.

Home Sweet Home

We were living large. I didn't know how much money he made, but I felt like a rich kid on this trip. I was only a teenager, but I understood I was seeing some things that most kids from Alabama would never see. But I was still a teenager. I didn't truly appreciate the moment.

Even though I was so happy that I was with my real father, a slow resentment began to build inside of me, and I didn't even know it. My goodness, I was still a kid in high school.

Honestly, I was a punk teenager. Because of all that had happened in my life, I had grown into a disrespectful jerk at times. On this trip, that side of me came out on several occasions.

I remember one time at a rest stop in Texas. I was tired and hot. My father told me to get out of the camper and come inside with them. I snapped back, "No, I am staying here." He replied, "Boy, don't talk to me that way. I am your father." Before even thinking about it, I yelled at him, "You may be my father, but you don't have any right to tell me anything. I'll come when I'm ready. Now leave me alone!" He slammed the door and left.

That event was a microcosm of the trip home. It began to escalate. Everyone just wanted to get home. It was so much driving, and we were all ill and frustrated. What had started out as a dream trip was beginning to feel like a prison. I just decided to keep my cassette player on full blast in my ears and ignore it all.

Eventually, we made it home. The trailer was so long, he had to pull it down into the driveway of my grandmother's house at the bottom of the hill. We all got out, and my brother and I headed towards the house. My father yelled to us, "Where do you think you're going? We have to unload this stuff."

Suitcases, leftover food, coolers, and much more were unloaded.

I remember thinking for a moment: "Did this really just happen?" I still couldn't believe the events of my life. I knew that my real father and I had hit some pretty big bumps on our trip, but it was going to be OK. I had found my father; my father had found his son. I wondered where we would go on our next family trip.

Never in my wildest dreams did I expect what would happen next.

Dropped and Broken

The relentless pursuit of David by Saul would eventually consume this once-great king. He would serve out the remaining years of his life in battle after battle.

During those years, David remained out of his way. He purposefully stayed back and quietly grew stronger. His group of ragtag men slowly developed a reputation of legend and devotion! Yet David did not pursue the kingdom. He would not tear the roots away from the kingdom of Saul. He still loved him and his son, Jonathan.

King Saul and Jonathan fought many battles together. It came to pass one day that they were both killed in battle together. Saul was wounded by an arrow and realized he was not going to make it, so he fell on his own sword and ended his life.

No one in the house of Saul expected that. They were probably prepared for the death of Saul; he was becoming an old man. But no one in their house expected both Saul and Jonathan to be killed on the same day.

Jonathan's son, Mephibosheth, was in the palace of the king that day. When the news arrived of the battle, there was the normal panic of the house. How many were killed or wounded? They were used to the casualties of war. But this day was different.

The messenger announced that both King Saul and Jonathan were dead. The news continued, "And even now, the enemy's forces are advancing towards the palace."

Mephibosheth's nurse watched as many of the soldiers charged with protecting the palace fled for their lives. She knew the Philistines would come for the next in line to the throne— Mephibosheth. So she picked the boy up and ran with him in her arms. She was trying to escape the palace and keep the next king safe.

It was one thing for his father and grandfather to be dead, but he still had a destiny of greatness ahead of him. The nurse just needed to get him to safety, and everything would be OK. But everything doesn't always work out as planned. The Word of God explains what happened next to this five-year-old boy.

"And it happened, as she made haste to flee, that he fell and became lame. His name was Mephibosheth" (2 Samuel 4:4).

Just like that, it went from bad to worse. Mephibosheth fell out of her arms and became lame in his feet. He instantly became paralyzed. No king could serve in this condition. It was over. All the dreams of Saul and Jonathan were over. In one day, the house of Saul was dead and gone forever. The little boy became famous, not because of a wise reign, but because of this utter tragedy.

In one day, the house of Saul was dead and gone forever. The little boy became famous, not because of a wise reign, but because of this utter tragedy.

The news of the death of Saul and Jonathan reached David. Many of his house were rejoicing, for they knew it was finally time for David to become king. But David was devastated. A part of him died that day, too.

Even so, David was a redwood, and his roots were connected to Jonathan. In his eyes, the mighty had fallen. He had no idea what had happened to that little boy then, but he would know of him one day.

Love and Like

When everything was finally unloaded from the camper, we were all exhausted. Everyone just wanted to go inside and crash. But my "real father" wanted to talk to me.

I remember thinking, "This is going to be our first father-and-son teaching moment." Even though I was aggravated because of a few things from the trip, I was glad to have a father that wanted to talk to me, and not scream at me or abuse me.

I prepared myself for a good "talking to," and then we would go forward. I was not prepared for what he said.

"Son, I want to tell you that I don't appreciate you talking back to me the way you did on this trip. You acted like a punk. I am not going to be talked to this way. I will not accept it."

"I'm sorry," I said. "I really am."

He said, "Well, I accept your apology, but you need to know where we stand as we go forward."

I said, "What does that mean?" His next words would cut me to the core.

"I love your mother. I always have and I always will. Well, I don't know how to say this, except to just come right out and say it. I love you as my son, but I don't like you! I don't know where this is going from this point forward."

I didn't know the story of Mephibosheth at that early age of my life, but I look back now and I realize that the same thing that happened to him had just happened to me.

The very one I had counted on to protect me had just dropped me.

I was dropped. I was broken. I was damaged goods. Nothing I had planned was ever going to happen. It was just not in the cards for me. It was a pipe dream.

The very one I had counted on to protect me had just dropped me.

Two fathers; two rejections.

He drove off that day and it was over. He contacted my mother a few times after that. But the bottom line was that my "dream dad" couldn't handle this "punk teenager." He was gone.

How does a teenage boy recover from that on his own? He doesn't.

A Place Called Lo Debar

When Mephibosheth's nurse realized what had happened to him, she knew she had to take him to a place he would never be found. She knew the soldiers would not rest until he was killed. The place she ended up taking him was called Lo Debar. Why do you think she chose this place? The word "Lo Debar" means "a place of no pasture, no hope, total desolation." Surely, no one would ever look in a place like that. This was no place for a king to live—even a broken king.

Lo Debar was probably one of the most isolated and lonely places in the known world. No one ever visited Lo Debar. You couldn't accidentally turn into the Lo Debar neighborhood. You had to make a conscious decision to leave hope, and walk or ride to its desolation.

Mephibosheth could not take care of himself. His nurse made sure that a family took him in and raised him. They were assigned to protect him, even into adulthood. Up until age five, he was waited on hand and foot. He had every luxury possible. But now, he was reduced to mere survival. He could not feed himself, use the bathroom by himself, or even bathe himself. One of the worst pains was the reality that his physical condition was now a burden to others, too.

When we are experiencing this type of loneliness and worthlessness, the enemy swoops in and brings the worst pain of all. He will tell you, "This is not about you anymore. You are dragging down the quality of life of everyone around you."

I want you to hear me on this!

This is a lie of the Devil. It is an attempt to make you end it all. He will tell you that everyone would be better off without you. *That is a lie*!

Let me pause for just a minute and speak personally. Many who are reading this book can identify with Mephibosheth. You have been broken and dropped by those you were supposed to be able to trust. You feel like your potential is gone. You think your life is worthless and that you will never do anything great for God.

Isolation and pity are tools of our Enemy. They are his attempt to take your eyes off a loving God and put them back on yourself. If Satan can convince you that God doesn't care about you, then you will surely not care about yourself, either.

Isolation and pity are tools of our Enemy. They are his attempt to take your eyes off a loving God and put them back on yourself.

The name Mephibosheth means "one who destroys shame!" Wow, the very thing he was named at birth to destroy was slowly destroying him. That is what Lo-Debar will do to you. That is what being dropped by someone you love will do, too.

The Spiral

Two fathers, two rejections. One abused me both physically and mentally; one destroyed my hopes and dreams of finding Super Dad.

You can probably guess what happened next in my life: I determined in my heart that I did not need a father. I could do this on my own. I decided to get lost in the teenager life.

For the next two years, I covered my pain with sports, girls, and being plain stupid. I was never a drug addict, or even drank in high school, but I was lost. I was in a very public Lo Debar.

I was fairly popular, but most of it was a front I put on to mask the pain inside. I was slowly turning into the men who had dropped and broken me.

I had often said, "I'll never be like him when I grow up. I know that for sure!" But, in my judgment of my two dads, and as a result of my pain and hurt, I was becoming the very person I said I would never be. I became selfish, prideful, irresponsible, and even disrespectful to the only person who had ever fought for me—my mother. I lied to her, took advantage of her, and even screamed at her. This is the part of my past of which I am most ashamed.

My emotions eventually turned to anger. Once I got so mad, I punched my fist through my bedroom door. My mother screamed at me, "You are becoming more and more like your father!" I screamed, "*Never!*" and stormed out of the room. But I knew in my heart she was right. I felt completely helpless to stop it. I didn't know how to change. This was all I had ever known.

You Can't Teach Size

Through the grace of God, and the grace of my teachers, I graduated high school (just barely). I wasn't dumb; I just didn't care. High school was only about football and my friends. Nothing else. My dream was to be a coach. Nothing in my life satisfied me like football. I think part of it was the ability to release my rage and not get in trouble for it.

I had tried out for a junior college team in Mississippi. I was offered a potential scholarship to play right out of high school. I remember thinking, "This is my shot to put all this behind me and make my own way." I had not applied myself to studying in high school, but I was determined to reach my full potential in college.

I kissed my mother goodbye and told all my friends I would see them later. I headed to Mississippi.

Through summer drills, I worked my way up to second string. This gigantic lineman from Mississippi was always right in front of me. I would destroy him every time. I was proud of myself. I was on the right track. Things were finally looking up for me.

One evening there was a knock on my dormitory door. "Larry, we need to talk." I had no idea what it could be about because I knew I was doing well on the field. "Son, I hate to say this, but we are going to have to cut you. I know you have done great, but you are one of our few out-of-state scholarships, and they are much more expensive to the college. There are some other guys on the team who are twice your size, but only half your talent and heart. But those boys are from Mississippi, so we can work with that. Son, I can teach them your skills, but I can't teach you their size. We have to let you go."

Dropped again!

Now I had to deal with the shame of coming back home just before fall semester and explaining to everyone why I had been cut from the team. I remember speeding on my way home. Of course, I was stopped by a Mississippi state trooper and given a ticket.

Just Give It to Jesus

Shockingly, I was over the shame of being cut very quickly once I got home. I just jumped right back into the old Larry. I was wasting my life away. My life consisted of "cruising" around our small town and hanging out in the local parking lot with my friends. But one night of hanging out would change everything.

This one particular girl was always hounding me to come to her church. I had no desire to be in any church. I had been raised in church and watched my dad pretend to be something he was not. Before we even got out of the parking lot on the way home on a Sunday morning, he was cussing the preacher, the singers, and all of us.

But she would not stop asking. Finally, just to shut her up, I told her I would go to the youth group night. Of all places, it turned out to be the same little church where I used to play the drums. Some of the same people even remembered me.

I went that night and felt something I hadn't felt in a long time. I felt like there was something there that I needed in my life. After that night, I kept going, and eventually started coming on Sundays, too, but I was still only coming to hang out with friends.

That is, until the night I crossed the line with my mother one too many times.

The real Larry continued to manifest his nasty self in the privacy of my childhood home. I was pretending to be someone in church that I was not in my private life. My mother knew I was just playing a game.

It wasn't the first time I had hurt my mother. I had let her down on many occasions. But most of the time I could talk my way out of it.

That night, she did something I never dreamed she would do. My mother kicked me out of the house. But this time I hadn't been dropped. She didn't break me or drop me. I had dropped myself.

The following week I lived in my little truck. I was homeless. I was at the bottom. I was alone.

One night I was sitting in my truck, contemplating what kind of man I had become. I replayed my whole life over and over in my head. I began to talk out loud to God. Honestly, I really don't know what I said. I just know I was honest with Him.

The following week I lived in my little truck. I was homeless. I was at the bottom. I was alone.

Suddenly, I felt the love of God come into my truck. I began to cry like I had not cried since I was a child. Something began to rise up in me. I was overwhelmed by the love of God. I sat up and cried out, "I give up, God. I surrender!"

That next day was Sunday. When the music started, I ran to the altar. I didn't wait on anyone to call me forward. I didn't care what the protocol was. I was ready to surrender. I didn't know what else to do.

I remember kneeling down, and thinking, "God, I don't know what to say." At that moment, one of the elders of the church came and prayed for me. I heard him say, "Son, you are home. Just give it to Jesus."

I did.

Is There No One Left of The House of Saul?

When David was finally about to sit on the throne of a unified Israel as king, he asked a very important question: "Is there still anyone who is left of the house of Saul, that I may show him kindness for Jonathan's sake?" (2 Samuel 9:1).

He was a Big Picture redwood king! He never cut the roots that connected him to those he honored, and he wanted to see the Big Picture in every situation. He was told there was a servant in the house named Ziba who had served Jonathan, so he was called to stand before the king. David said to him, "'Are you Ziba?' He said, 'At your service!'" (2 Samuel 9:2b).

"Then the king said, 'Is there not still someone of the house of Saul, to whom I may show the kindness of God?' And Ziba said to the king,

'There is still a son of Jonathan who is lame in his feet.' So the king said to him, 'Where is he?' And Ziba said to the king, 'Indeed he is in the house of Machir the son of Ammiel, in Lo Debar.' Then King David sent and brought him out of the house of Machir the son of Ammiel, from Lo Debar" (2 Samuel 9:3–5).

David could not imagine sitting down on his throne without honoring the covenant he had made with Jonathan. Jonathan had known that God had chosen David to be the next king instead of him, so he made David promise to show kindness to his house when he entered into his kingdom (see 1 Samuel 20:13–16).

David could not imagine sitting down on his throne without honoring the covenant he had made with Jonathan.

When Mephibosheth arrived, they laid him on the floor in front of David. "Mephibosheth?" David asked. "Yes, my Lord, I am your servant." David told the guards to hold him up. What happened next teaches us that it is never over.

"So David said to him, 'Do not fear, for I will surely show you kindness for Jonathan your father's sake, and will restore to you all the land of Saul your grandfather; and you shall eat bread at my table continually'" (2 Samuel 9:7).

He was completely restored by King David. Everything that was lost the day he was dropped, was restored in *one moment*. This was only possible because of the favor of the king! He went on to say, "You will eat at my table from this day forward! You are royalty!"

Mephibosheth heard David, but he didn't believe him. Just like the children of Israel had come out of Egypt but couldn't get Egypt out of themselves, Mephibosheth couldn't shake Lo Debar from his mind. All he could see was a crippled man that had let everyone down.

He replied, "What is your servant, that you should look upon such a dead dog as I?" (2 Samuel 9:8). In his mind, he was already dead.

But David was about to become a father to Mephibosheth and restore everything to him.

David ended the proclamation by saying, "As for Mephibosheth … he will eat at my table like one of the king's sons" (2 Samuel 9:11). And he did for the rest of his life.

You don't have to physically make a child to be a father. I had two that tried, and two that dropped me. But God was about to finally send me fathers that would never leave me, and never drop me, again.

The Night Bowling Changed My Life

I had surrendered my life to Jesus that night at the altar, and things began to change for me. I reconciled with my mother and was allowed to move back home. Things were going in a better direction.

I was no longer trying to mask my insecurities by pretending to be someone I wasn't. I was looking for the real thing. I still had much bitterness and unforgiveness towards both my dads, but I was moving on. Like Mephibosheth, I was slowly being restored. I was being rebuilt by God through genuine relationships in my local church.

I was becoming more and more involved in the youth and young adult groups. From time to time, they would have fun activities for us to go to outside of church. On one particular night, they told us we were going bowling. I wasn't too excited about it. I didn't really like to bowl.

But I was sort of liking one of the girls in the youth group, and I thought it would be cool to hang out with her and the rest of the gang. I can truly say that God can use anything to steer your life in the direction of your purpose and destiny. I didn't know it at the time, but God was using a bowling alley to reveal greatness in me!

As I sat down around the ball return for our team, laughing and joking and having a good time, something caught my attention out of the corner of my eye. Actually, it was "someone."

In the alley next to us was a beautiful blonde from our youth group. I knew her casually, but that night something told me: *She is the one for you!* I instantly felt drawn to her. I am ashamed to say that I left the one I was with and joined "her" team! Actually, I'm really glad I did!

I have no idea how well or horrible I played that night at the bowling alley. I didn't care. My heart was racing for this cute little blonde. Little did I know that she would be the one God would use *to restore all things to me* and *see greatness in me*!

Not long after that night, I would be telling my lifelong best friend (who was in the youth group, too): "I'm gonna marry that girl. You watch me. I'm gonna marry her!"

Chapter Five

Rubber Band Revelation

Do You Love Me or Not?

Sandy and I started dating, and I quickly fell in love. She was much more reluctant to say those three magical words than I was. In fact, as our relationship quickly grew, I would constantly tell her, "I love you." She would reply with some variation of "Thank you! That is so sweet!"

I'm not gonna lie; it was a blow to my ego. But I was determined to not let her slip away. I was going to "win" her heart. She didn't know it yet, but I already had a life planned with her. I was already determined she would take my last name.

One night, after a few months of my many "I love yous" without the desired response, I decided I'd had enough.

I had pulled in the driveway of her parents' house. I was standing by my car door, and I said, "Sandy, I love you!" She once again said something like, "And I care for you a lot." I was so angry, I responded, "Sandy, I am getting in this car and never coming back if you don't tell me exactly how you feel about me. Do you love me or not?" She looked at me with what I call that "patented Sandy smile" and said, "Of course, I love you, Larry!"

Boom! I knew at that moment that I had just won the heart of my soulmate! I didn't know then that God was setting us up for greatness—together.

She was the first person to whom I ever told my dreams. She was the first person with whom I felt I could share all my brokenness, shame, rejection, and even hopes. She was my "dream girl."

The Coat of Favor

One of my absolute favorite characters in the Bible is Joseph (of the Old Testament). You probably know him by his "coat of many colors." But he was about so much more than that.

Joseph was a dreamer. He dreamed in the natural realm (in his sleep), and he had dreams for his future, too.

God had big plans for Joseph.

You may not realize this, but there is more Scripture dedicated to the story of Joseph than there is to Abraham, Isaac, and Jacob. And in these verses, there is not one word of rebuke from God. There is not one reference to Joseph losing his integrity or his commitment to God.

Joseph loved God, and he loved his family. Unfortunately, that love was not reciprocated. His brothers were jealous of their father's love for him. They constantly tried to find ways to speak down to him and degrade his self-worth.

One day, after being with his brothers, he came home to his father. Jacob (Joseph's father) could tell something was wrong with his son. He asked him what had happened. Joseph reported how his brothers had treated him. It was at that point that one of the most famous stories in the Bible transpired. There is even a Broadway musical named after it that has been performed since 1968. Of course, the musical is not exactly theologically sound.

Even if someone has never read the Bible, they have heard of the "coat of many colors"; they may not know all that happened to Joseph, but they certainly know about that coat!

Jacob made the coat for his son because he could see the rejection in his face. Joseph's brothers had mocked him and ridiculed him, but Joseph only wanted to fit in with them. Instead, his brothers resented him; they were jealous of the favor their father showed him.

The Bible tells us that Jacob loved Joseph more than any of his sons because he was born to his true love, Rachel. She had passed away, and whenever Jacob looked at Joseph he saw her. He felt compelled to lavish him with favor.

So he made him a special coat—a coat made of many colors of cloth. It was surely a sight to see. It would have caused him to stand out in any crowd. It was the one thing he didn't need to wear when he saw his brothers. The coat made his brothers hate him even more. It caused them to speak more evil against him. The seeds of bitterness gave root to revenge.

But that night, Joseph had a dream.

The Truth Always Comes Out

I had been dropped by two different fathers. I was damaged goods. I was broken. In many ways, I was a fraud. Somehow, I had convinced the prettiest girl in school to fall in love with me. It felt like a dream. I didn't want to wake up; but we always wake up, and the dream is over.

The many seeds of hurt and disappointment from my fathers had produced a rotten-fruit tree. The broken and dropped boy had now become a broken and dropped man. My idea of what a true man looked like was convoluted and awry. I was destined to ruin any dream I had for my life. It was inevitable.

The many seeds of hurt and disappointment from my fathers had produced a rotten-fruit tree. The broken and dropped boy had now become a broken and dropped man.

I had no sense of responsibility. Without a father in my life to teach me what a good man does, I just made it up on my own as I went along. Of course, this was a disaster.

Sandy didn't know that I had already accumulated a sizable amount of debt. At my young age, I had already had a truck repossessed and several bills that had not been paid and were turned over to collection agencies.

I didn't know it at the time, but I was still trying to win the love of those I so desired to love me. Whatever money I had, I spent it on dates with Sandy, buying her gifts, and making her think she was with a man who "had it all together." Sadly, that was the furthest thing from the truth.

On Christmas Eve of 1988, I asked Sandy to marry me. She enthusiastically said yes! My dream was happening.

In my mind, I had pulled it off. I was not trying to be tricky and lie to her. I really believed I had changed.

I remember hearing someone say, "Sometimes God will bless your mess." Of course, I was standing on that word! I found out quickly though that the truth was "whatever a man sows, that he will also reap" (Galatians 6:7).

Just a couple of months before our planned wedding, we signed a lease to rent a mobile home. I moved in and started working on it. One day, Sandy was there painting and working on some other things. She realized it was getting a little late and needed to go back home. She picked up the phone to call her mom and tell her she was coming (yes, this was the "old days" when we had landlines). But there was a problem. There was no dial tone.

"Larry, what is wrong with the phone? It's not working," she said. My reflex response almost caused me to lie to her, and make up some crazy excuse, but I was tired of running. I said, "I didn't pay the bill. I guess they cut it off."

That was not a good night. The dead phone line caused me to confess all the things from my irresponsible life to her. I told her about everything I had not paid and everything I had lost. My credit was as low as you can possibly go.

She looked at me and said, "I am not going to live this way. This is not the life I have planned. We are going to sit down with my parents and make a budget. We are going to get out of this mess. We are going to fix this. But, Larry, you will not keep anything from me ever again. I must know everything. If we are going to make this work, I have to know everything."

Over the next few days, I peeled layer after layer off the onion that was my life. Just like an onion brings tears when it is being cut, there were many shed. But for the first time in my life, I had told someone everything. I had come clean: the good, the bad and the ugly. Just like Joseph, I told her my dreams, but I also shared the nightmares I had lived.

Unlike Joseph's brothers, she didn't hate me or try to hurt me because of my dreams and nightmares. She loved me; she forgave me, and she helped me.

Our conversations during our engagement set the foundation for that dreadful day at city hall in my small town. The day I would stand in shame before a judge. The day Sandy would somehow see greatness in me. God used this eighteen-year-old girl to show me His favor. Her love was my coat of many colors!

The Invasion of the Dream Snatchers

Joseph laid his head down that night and went to sleep. He was exhausted from the long trip to see his brothers. But more than anything, he was emotionally exhausted from the pain his jealous brothers had put on him.

I am sure he probably tossed, turned, and struggled to go to sleep. Have you ever been in a place where you were exhausted bodily, but your mind couldn't seem to settle down and let you rest? You close your eyes and hope to go to sleep so you can forget the events of the day, but your mind will just not let it go. We finally go to sleep, only to be tormented with nightmares about the situation we are facing. This was not the case for Joseph on this evening.

Once he finally dozed off, God gave him a very specific dream. This dream was unlike any he had ever had before. It would be a dream of destiny, purpose, and the survival of a nation.

When he had his first dream, he did the one thing he probably didn't need to do. He told his brothers. He was so innocent in his thinking that he really believed his brothers would be happy for him.

They said, "OK, tell us your dream." Joseph said, "In my dream, we were all in the field binding bundles of wheat. Then suddenly, my bundle stood up and then all of yours bowed down to my bundle of wheat" (Genesis 37:5–7, author's paraphrase).

Of course, they answered, "That is so amazing, Joseph. We're so glad you told us your dream. We are so excited about submitting our lives to you and serving you. Joseph, you are the man!" Not! They hated him even more for his dream.

That night, Joseph dreamed another dream. But this time, he went to his brothers and his father. "See if you like this dream. It is even more amazing! In my second dream, all twelve of us brothers were stars. Dad was the sun and Mom was the moon. Suddenly, the other eleven stars (you guys), and the sun and moon (Mom and Dad), bowed down to me (my star). Isn't that cool?" (Genesis 37:9–11, author's paraphrase).

Jacob spoke up and said, "Son, what kind of dream is this? Are you saying that me and your momma, and all your brothers, are going to serve you? What did you eat last night, boy?" Interestingly, his brothers hated and envied him, but his father "kept the matter in mind" (Genesis 37:11).

Here is a simple principle that can make or break your future: be careful who you share your dreams with!

The dream was for Joseph. The dream wasn't for his brothers or for his father. They were the focus of the dream, but it was not their dream. It was Joseph's dream.

Many may remember the movie where aliens came to Earth and stole the identities of humans, then grew their replacement bodies from pods in the ground. They would become zombielike replicas of the humans. They "stole their bodies." They "snatched" their lives from them.

This is exactly what will happen if you tell your dreams to the wrong person. They will invade your world and steal your dream. They will do everything they can to stop it from happening. Be careful who you tell your dreams to. Not everyone is going to be excited about what the Lord has told you.

Be careful who you tell your dreams to.
Not everyone is going to be excited about
what the Lord has told you.

Here is another principle that you need to get deep in your spirit. Your God-given dream will always be to help or serve others. It will be your dream, but its focus will be saving the lives of others.

I have always believed the "coat of many colors" was symbolic of many nations and peoples. I don't think Jacob even realized the significance of his gesture of love and favor to his son. That coat was a preview to Joseph's dream. It spoke of the many nations and cultures his son would save one day.

Joseph's desire to serve his brothers was the seed that would bring the dream to fruition. You may have heard the saying, "What you make happen for others, God will make happen for you." This is precisely the story of Joseph. He served everywhere he went. No matter who dropped him, he served them.

The "hopeless dreamer" with the strange coat just kept on loving and serving, but his brothers decided they'd had enough of the dreamer and plotted to crush his dream once and for all. They decided to snatch his dream away from him forever.

Preaching to the Squirrels and Birds

How could I have ever known that the church I circled on my bike as a young boy would become the church in which I would watch my bride walk down the aisle to marry me?

We were joined in holy matrimony in May of that year. Just a couple of kids thinking they had big plans for their lives. We were both working decent jobs and had moved into a simple mobile home on the land where my grandparents had once lived.

We had brought all my debt and mistakes into the marriage, but it was all out in the open. No secrets. We had a plan to slowly pay it off and restore my credit. We had a dream. We had a plan.

What neither one of us realized was that God had a vision for us, too. His vision was not what we had planned.

As I said, we were married in May. By August of that same year, we were working in ministry. Just like the day I knocked on the former pastor's door and asked to be the drummer, I knocked on the new pastor's door and asked to be the youth pastor. It was the same door of the same parsonage.

We had zero experience, but we had a dream. Somewhere deep inside of me, it had always been there.

I look back over my life now, and I realize that God had always given me dreams about doing something great. I would share those dreams with people in my life, people who should have helped me walk into them. But instead, those people just dropped me again. Over time, my dreams were stolen.

As a child, I had a great desire to serve God. I would watch my father sing on the stage of our little church, and the power of God would fall. People would respond to his singing in a mighty way.

I remember being drawn to the music and the stage. I wanted to be up there with my dad. On a few occasions, my brother and I sang backup on one of his songs. Well, we didn't really sing backup. We would sing one word. There was an Easter song about the Resurrection he often sang. The lyrics of the chorus were, "Gone, the stone is rolled back. Gone, the tomb is empty. Gone, to sit at the Father's side…" and our part was, "Gone!" That was it. That was our fifteen seconds of fame.

Unfortunately, though, my desire to serve God in music turned to a bitterness toward it. This was the result of seeing my dad act one way on the stage only to curse the preacher and others before we left the church parking lot. I was determined to not play the "church game."

When I rebelled in high school, I really rebelled. I didn't want to go to church. The ministry was the furthest thing from my mind. But God had a dream for me and Sandy that was truly unexpected.

We were satisfied with youth ministry. That's as far as we were willing to go. But then something strange started happening to me. I started to have dreams of myself preaching before large crowds, many times, in other countries.

But then something strange started happening to me. I started to have dreams of myself preaching before large crowds.

Not long after that, I took our youth group to a Christian concert. In the middle of the concert, the singer stopped singing and started preaching. The lead singer looked at the crowd and said, "It's time to stop running! It is time to submit to the voice of God." I was so scared. I said to myself, "If this is really what you want me to do, I need you to show me tonight!"

As soon as the band started back playing music, a great friend who I had known and respected for many years leaned forward and said, "Larry, the Lord said it is time for you to preach the gospel. Those dreams you have been having are from God!"

I started crying and said, "I surrender, God. I will no longer run from You. I will preach Your gospel to the world!" I found out quickly that God has a sense of humor. He also lays out strange paths for your destiny. I thought I would immediately have preaching engagements lined up. But shockingly, pastors were not lining up to book a sheetrock hanger/inexperienced youth pastor to preach for them.

There was a fire burning inside of me to preach! I couldn't wait for pastors to call me, so I decided to go outside and preach to the birds, squirrels, and rabbits. There was always an occasional dog or cat that wandered up and listened, too. I preached Holy Ghost and fire to those animals. Most of them left and went back in the woods, but I kept preaching.

Pit Happens

Joseph's brothers had a plan to shut the dreamer up for good. They decided to kill him and be done with it. If the dreamer was dead, his dream would be dead with him.

"Now when they saw him afar off, even before he came near them, they conspired against him to kill him. Then they said to one another, 'Look, this dreamer is coming! Come therefore, let us now kill him and cast him into some pit; and we shall say, "Some wild beast has devoured him." We shall see what will become of his dreams!'" (Genesis 37:18–20).

Just as they were about to grab him and kill him, the oldest brother (Reuben) spoke up and saved Joseph's life. His plan was to throw Joseph into a deep pit from which he couldn't climb out.

Scripture explains that Reuben was actually trying to fool the other brothers into thinking they were finally rid of Joseph. Instead he planned to come back and get him later and take him back home to his father (see Genesis 37:21–22).

Now I want you to get this. After throwing him in the pit, the Bible says the brothers sat down and had lunch. While their brother was in a pit, they were sitting on the side of the pit eating a sandwich. They were celebrating the death of the dreamer's dream.

About that time, one of the other brothers (Judah) saw a band of traders coming that way. He spoke up and said, “Let’s get rid of the dreamer for good. We can sell him to the traders. Then we could take this fancy coat and cover it in blood. When we take it back to our father, he will believe Joseph is dead!” (Genesis 37:25–28, author’s paraphrase).

So the brothers pulled Joseph from the pit and sold him to the traders for twenty pieces of silver. They took the bloody coat back to their father and said, “Do you have any idea who this coat belongs to?” Jacob saw it and proclaimed, “My son has been torn apart by a wild animal.” His grief was so strong, he wanted to die and be with Joseph (Genesis 37:31–35, author’s paraphrase).

We’ve all heard the verse “God works in mysterious ways,” haven’t we? The problem is that this is not in the Bible. This phrase is often cited to explain the workings of God. Although the intention of this manmade proverb is good, it is not completely accurate.

His ways are mysterious to us, but His ways in the kingdom are very intentional. God is always intentional. He never makes it up as He goes along. He is the Alpha and the Omega; He is the Beginning and the End. Therefore, He knew this was going to happen when He gave Joseph the dreams. He knew what the coat would be used for one day! In fact, God had to temporarily remove Reuben from the situation so that he couldn’t come back and save him. He didn’t need Joseph to go back to his father. God needed Joseph to be sold out of that pit. The dream was not going to happen in the land of Jacob. The dream was going to happen in Egypt.

The pit was a necessity to the future fulfillment of Joseph’s dreams.

God used this pit experience to produce the path to the dream. The pit was a necessity to the future fulfillment of Joseph’s dreams.

I remember a famous, or infamous, saying that became a bumper sticker. It was vulgar then, and still is now, but it summed up most people’s idea of life. I will certainly not repeat it here. But, it rhymed with “pit happens.” In this life, pit happens. It happens to all of us. But to the child of God, the pit has a purpose.

Without the pit, the promise couldn't have been fulfilled in Joseph's life. It is fascinating to me that through the entire pit experience, you never hear him fighting back. He embraced it as part of the plan for the promise.

I know that God didn't throw me into the pit. When both of my fathers rejected me and dropped me, I fell into a pit. The Enemy designed that pit of depression and lack of self-worth to kill me. But I wouldn't take anything for my journey! I wouldn't change a thing.

Without the pit experience of my life, I would have never come back to Christ. Without the pit, I would have never met and married Sandy. Without the pit, I would have never received the call to preach the gospel. Without the pit, I certainly wouldn't have ever written this book.

For Joseph, the pit had to happen. It is going to happen to you, too. It probably already has on some level.

But I am encouraging you to perceive the pit the way God wants you to see it. Yes, pit happens. It happens for a reason. It is to shape your purpose. It is to refine your praise. Remember this: Most people can't relate to your dreams—because your dreams are not their dreams. But most people *can* relate to your pit. Everyone has gone through some sort of pit. Someone has sold us all out, at one time or another. The dream snatchers are everywhere. They will throw you in a pit in a second.

But we must praise God in the pit because we know it is the path to the palace.

The Journey Begins

Not long after my powerful church services with the animals at the edge of the woods, I finally got to preach in an actual pulpit.

We continued to be the youth pastors at our church for a little while longer. This was one of the most pivotal times of our lives. We learned many things in youth ministry that we still use in our ministry today.

In just a short while, God called us out to start our first church. We had a very small group of people with us. Barely enough to fill a small living room. In fact, that is where our first service was. I set up a barstool in the living room of my wife's parents' home and preached a world-changing message called: "What Kind of Tree Are You?" It lasted about ten minutes. But I got a few amens.

It wasn't long before we outgrew meeting in houses, and we knew we needed a building. There was an old, abandoned storefront building in the middle of our small town. It had not been used in decades. In fact, it had no roof and no floor. It was just four brick walls open to the sky! Grass and weeds as tall as a man were growing up through the dirt floor. But when I walked in it, my eyes opened to the spirit realm.

It was my first taste of vision. I could see the stage and where my pulpit would be. I saw the metal chairs and the middle aisle that guests would walk down. I saw it all, and I began to walk it out for our few church people who were with us that day. I was so excited, and I just knew they would be excited, too. They were excited. But they could not see what I could see. It was more than a dream. It was a vision.

Joseph's dream came to him in his sleep, therefore it was perceived as a dream. But a dream will not sustain you through challenging times. Only vision can do that. Joseph's dream was really a vision.

A dream will not sustain you through challenging times. Only vision can do that. Joseph's dream was really a vision.

I was young and didn't know what was happening. I now know that God was planting a vision in that small town that would sustain me through some of the most challenging moments of my life. The vision helped me to clearly see the path God had before us. It would take us on a journey that I would have never dreamed possible. But that is what vision is. Vision is always bigger than you. It is always impossible. It never works exactly the way you thought it would.

Running for Your Life

Joseph was pulled from the pit and sold to the traveling merchants. Once they reached Egypt, they peddled Joseph at a horrible slave auction. Rich people would come and "shop" for the best-looking, strongest male. A man named Potiphar was drawn to Joseph and purchased him to serve in his home.

Joseph quickly impressed Potiphar with his dedication and integrity. Soon Potiphar began to see that Joseph's God had blessed him greatly. He noticed there was a direct correlation to the added prosperity of his house and the fact that Joseph was there.

As the days went by, Potiphar began to show "favor" to Joseph and trust him with all his possessions. So much so, that he turned all his finances over to him as well. The Bible says Potiphar didn't even "know what he had except for the bread which he ate" (Genesis 39:6).

Joseph was a very good-looking guy. He was probably well-built, too, as a result of all the demanding work he had done most of his life. More than that—the anointing and the favor of God is also attractive. Potiphar's wife became fascinated with Joseph. Her fascination quickly turned to lust.

On many occasions, she asked Joseph to sleep with her, but he refused each time. He said, "Look, my master does not know what is with me in the house, and he has committed all that he has to my hand. There is no one greater in this house than I, nor has he kept back anything from me but you, because you are his wife. How then can I do this great wickedness, and sin against God?" (Genesis 39:8–9).

His integrity wouldn't let him give in. His dream was too big. His vision kept him focused on the promise. He had already come too far to throw it all away in a moment. It was just too big. It was not all about him. His dream was about God using him to do a magnificent work in his family.

Every visionary must be vigilant to watch for these dream snatchers. They will follow you in all phases of your dream.

Potiphar's wife was another dream snatcher in the life of a visionary.

Every visionary must be vigilant to watch for these dream snatchers. They will follow you in all phases of your dream. They will come in different forms, but their goal is the same: they want you to abandon your dream.

Mrs. Potiphar was so angry at his last rejection that she pulled Joseph's clothes off him. Surely, this was going to be enough for him to give her what she wanted. But instead, the dream inside of Joseph told him to run! And run he did!

Sometimes, the only way to preserve the vision and your integrity is to run. Running isn't always a sign of weakness. Many times, it is a sign of wisdom.

Sometimes, the only way to preserve the vision and your integrity is to run.

Potiphar's wife was still holding Joseph's clothes. She was angry and offended, and her pride was bruised. I am sure Joseph was not the first young man she went after when Potiphar was away. He was just the first one to tell her no. Her response was immediate. "Someone help me! Please someone come and help me. Joseph has attacked me and tried to force me to lay with him" (Genesis 39:13–18, author's paraphrase).

Later that day Potiphar came home, and she told him the lie that she had created. She falsely accused an innocent man. But Potiphar believed his wife, and immediately he threw Joseph into prison.

The dream had taken another unexpected detour. Initially, the promise had taken him to a pit. The pit had taken him to Potiphar's house. Potiphar's house had taken him to prison. But in Joseph's heart, the dream was still alive.

From the Prison to the Palace

The favor of God would follow Joseph even in the prison cell. His integrity went before him. Even the warden of the jail could see there was something special about Joseph.

The Bible tells us that he was put in charge of taking care of the other prisoners, even though he was a prisoner himself. He could basically come and go as he pleased. He had great favor.

One day, he was approached by a couple of fellow inmates. One was the chief baker of the king, and the other was the chief cupbearer of the king. They had both committed offenses to the kingdom and had been thrown in jail for punishment. They both needed help interpreting dreams from the previous night. Joseph could see they were very troubled. He was glad to listen and take their dreams to God for the interpretation.

When they told him their dreams, he interpreted both of them. The dreams had to do with them being released from prison. One was an exciting dream, and the other "not so exciting."

Joseph told the cupbearer that he would be released and restored to the king's side. Sadly, the baker was told that he would be killed by the king. Joseph asked the cupbearer, "Please remember me when you are standing with Pharaoh. Can you give me a good word? Anything that will help me get out of here. I have done nothing to deserve this" (Genesis 40:14–15, author's paraphrase).

It happened just like Joseph said it would happen. But when the cupbearer was restored, he forgot about Joseph.

As time went by, Pharaoh himself dreamed two dreams that also troubled him greatly. He called for his sorcerers to interpret them, and they could not. At that moment, the cupbearer remembered Joseph! He told Pharaoh about all that had happened in the jail.

Word was sent to the prison to retrieve Joseph and bring him before the king. He cleaned himself up and prepared for his moment. He knew this was the fulfillment of the dream he had held onto throughout his life.

As Pharaoh told him the dreams, God immediately anointed Joseph to interpret them. God used Joseph to warn Pharaoh of a massive famine that would be coming in seven years, but the dreams also told him that he had seven years to prepare.

The answer made Pharaoh very happy. Therefore, Joseph's reputation was elevated in the eyes of the most powerful man in the world. His record was expunged. He was free. He promoted Joseph to his second-in-command leadership position on the spot. In one day, Joseph went from a prison cell to a palace throne. He was placed in charge of all the grain and food of Egypt.

When the famine hit the land, Jacob (Joseph's father) and his family was hit hard. They heard of the abundance of grain in Egypt and went to buy as much as they could. Through the course of many amazing encounters, Joseph's brothers were made aware that Joseph was the distributor of the grain. They were shocked. He did not resemble himself at all. They had believed he was dead.

It was an emotional reunion to say the least.

When they realized it was Joseph, and that he was alive, they feared for their lives. But Joseph was focused on the Big Picture. He knew this was the dream. He was leading his brothers, and even his father, just like the dreams said he would. But he didn't care about that. What mattered most to him was that the dream meant he would be able to save his family from starvation. It had never been about him!

Joseph was able to hold onto his dream because he was a visionary. He knew his purpose. He would not allow himself to be defined by a pit, or a prison, or even a palace.

It was a long journey. But, his family was together again. The "dreamer" was living the dream!

The Differences between Purpose, Vision, and Destiny

Many believe that our purpose, dreams, vision, and even destiny are the same, or interchangeable. This couldn't be further from the truth. Understanding the differences can be a life saver.

Purpose is the reason you were created. Everything that has ever been made, was designed with a purpose. God designed us, and He had a purpose in mind. Our purpose was stated in our creation.

"Then God said, 'Let Us make man in Our image, according to Our likeness; let them have dominion over the fish of the sea, over the birds of the air, and over the cattle, over all the earth and over every creeping thing that creeps on the earth" (Genesis 1:26).

He was very clear about our purpose. We were intended to operate in dominion over everything on this earth. Period. That's it. We were put here to govern the earth. We are all kings on this earth (our domain). This is why Jesus is known as the King of Kings. He is our King.

Some people say, "I want to find my destiny or purpose or vision for my life." But until you understand the differences, you will not find any of them.

Destiny is related to the word *destination*, so our destiny is where God plans for us to end up one day.

Vision is the game changer of them all. God's Word declares, "Where there is no vision, the people perish" (Proverbs 29:18 KJV). In other words, vision is very important.

I like to make things simple to understand, so let's make this as simple as possible.

Vision is a term we use for our eyesight. We go to the eye doctor to have our vision checked. Many of you have perfect 20/20 vision, while all the rest of us can't see without the aid of glasses or contacts. Some of you have even had surgery to correct your vision.

God's vision for your life is very similar. While purpose is *why* you were created, and destiny is *where* you are going, *vision is the ability to see and navigate your way*, from the why to the where.

While purpose is *why* you were created, and destiny is *where* you are going, *vision is the ability to see and navigate your way*, from the why to the where.

You can't get where you are going if you can't see where you're going. Therefore, the Word tells us we perish if we don't have vision. Without vision, you will walk off a cliff or into oncoming traffic.

I remember the first time I had to get glasses as an adult. I was working a full-time job and supporting my little family. I was studying and preaching as much as possible. I started getting headaches and having a little trouble seeing the text. Sandy said, "Larry, you have to get your eyes checked. I don't think you realize how blind you are!" I responded, "It is not that bad. I'll go, but I don't think I need glasses."

As I sat in that chair and heard the doctor say, "Which is better: A or B, 1 or 2?" I responded "A, 2, C, 1…," and in just a few minutes the world changed! I heard angels singing, "Alleluia!" I could see tiny little letters that I didn't even know were on the chart before.

The entire world changed that day. When I was driving home, I read every road sign out loud. I would say, "What? I was supposed to see that this soon?" I was looking at other cars and smiling like a goofball.

I didn't care. I could see where I was going. I had thought I could see before that, but I needed an adjustment.

And just like our eyes need to be checked and adjusted, as we get older, so does our vision.

When God first gives us the vision for our lives, we can only see what our spirit eyes are capable of processing in that season. He may give us snapshots of the future, but we are not ready to "see" the process we will need to take to get us there. If we could see all the pits and prisons that were taking us to the promise, we would certainly throw in the towel and say, "I can't do this."

Joseph had spiritual 20/20 vision. Through his integrity and faithfulness to God, the dream was always before him. No matter where he was, his vision let him clearly see where he was going. Our purpose is to walk and operate in dominion. Our destiny is our place of greatness in the kingdom. Vision will sustain us along the journey. I want to be a *vision man*.

Tents, Storefronts, Barns

The vision has taken us on a journey of a lifetime. I still can't believe all that God has done.

Our small group began to work on the abandoned building in our little town. We did all the work. Poured the concrete, built the rafters, and installed the roof. We ran the wiring and all the plumbing.

We were also introduced to our first experience of opposition and spiritual warfare. As we "handmade" our roof trusses during the day, vandals came in and destroyed them at night. On another occasion, someone ripped our church sign out of the ground. We were discouraged, but nothing was going to stop us. We had a vision!

Little did we know that God was preparing this small group of men and women to restore and rebuild many old abandoned buildings in the future.

I was now a senior pastor of my first church. I was twenty-three years old and clueless about what a pastor was supposed to be. We were in the restored building for a little over three years. Around that time, I felt a strong calling to the next level of my leadership and ministry. I didn't know what it was, but I felt it was time for a radical shift.

After much prayer, Sandy and I felt a calling to evangelism. The summer of that year, we launched our "tent ministry." We took the tent all over northern Alabama and had some of the greatest services we had ever experienced. At the end of the summer we conducted an eight-week revival, and over ninety people were saved.

During that revival, the vision was corrected again. I could finally see clearly what our church was supposed to look like. We had so many new believers in that revival. I talked to them about starting a church together. They were "all in."

In October of 1994, we established Solid Rock Church with the remnants of the eight-week tent revival. I am proud to say that many of those who were saved in that tent are still with us today.

During the years of ministry, we have moved from a tent, to a storefront, to a "little white building," and even to an old hay barn. The "old hay barn" period is legendary for us. It was our first purchase of any kind of property. It was in the country, and it was literally an old hay barn. Dirt floors and no walls. Only an old rusty, leaky tin roof. But, just like our first building, we had a vision for that old barn.

We drew out our plans with a stick in the dirt. We rolled up our sleeves and turned an old hay barn into a beautiful sanctuary, classrooms, and bathrooms. One hundred percent of the work was done by volunteers in our church. We've always said, "We serve, but we also work in this vision."

One day as we were leaving church, I couldn't find Sandy. I looked all through the church, but she was nowhere to be found. I went outside and there she was. On her knees, on the ground, outside of the hay barn. I said, "Sandy, are you OK? What are you doing?" She stood up, and with tears running down her cheeks, she showed me her hands. They were filled with dirt. Sandy then said, "This dirt runs through my veins. It is in me." That's how much this vision meant to Sandy. She was overwhelmed by it. The dirt was the vision. It was running through her veins!

We were there for a little over seven years. The vision was expanded and corrected many times to prepare us for what was coming.

Rubber Bands

The late Dr. Myles Munroe said it perfectly: "Where purpose is unknown, abuse is inevitable."[1]

> Where purpose is unknown,
> abuse is inevitable.

A lack of understanding of this principle is the foundation of a "visionless life." Many people, including myself, have spent years wandering in circles without any clear direction for their lives. Many of our wounds are self-inflicted. We are abusing ourselves daily because we have not taken the time to find our purpose. We can't see that purpose because our vision is not correct.

Knowing your purpose is directly tied to how well you can see yourself and your future vision.

Think about a key. It has a purpose. It was created to lock or unlock a door. Maybe its purpose was to start a car. If we use a key for a tiny pry bar, to open something that is stuck, it often bends and maybe even breaks. Then we get mad at the key. But the key is screaming back at you, "This is not my purpose! I was not created to do that." Where purpose is unknown, abuse is inevitable.

The purpose of a rubber band is only revealed when it is stretched! It can sit on the table and be called a rubber band. It can be in a package with 999 other rubber bands. The packaging says "rubber bands," but until they are taken out of the package and stretched, they will never find their purpose.

My heart for this book is to *stretch* you, and challenge you, to believe you can do more than you ever dreamed possible. All believers are rubber bands waiting to be stretched. The stretching is part of God's plan.

---

1. Munroe, Myles. 2001. *Understanding the Purpose and Power of Woman.* New Kensington, PA: Whitaker House.

Your stretching may be in a pit. But pit happens. Life is not about what happens to you. It is about how you respond to what happens to you. Joseph had to be stretched into his purpose.

All believers are rubber bands waiting to be stretched. The stretching is part of God's plan.

I, too, was about to be stretched tighter than I ever had been. But just as we will see with Joseph, it was God correcting my vision for me. I had to see beyond my comfort zone if I was going to be a world changer.

We are called to be world changers! But we are rubber bands first. We can't change the world in the package with all the other rubber bands. God has called us out of the pack and into His hands. He is the One who stretches us. As we close this chapter, I encourage you to take a moment and pray a simple prayer:

"Lord Jesus, I am ready to be stretched into my purpose. I know You will not take me down a path of destruction. You are with me no matter what I am going through. This is part of Your vision correctness over my life. I want to see clearly. I want to know where I am going. Here I am, Lord; use me, stretch me, mold me, fashion me, chisel me, and create a new heart in me, oh Lord!"

Now, let's stretch!

Chapter Six

Rebuilding the Old Waste Places

Cloudy Vision

God blessed us big time in the old hay barn, but it was a very difficult time for me and my family personally. The pressures of the ministry were becoming greater and greater. Finances were a major struggle, and I had begun to ponder how we were going to make it as a family and a ministry.

I cried out to God for inspiration, for a way to "stay in the game," and not quit. I had seen several pastors who I never dreamed would ever walk away from the ministry just give up and shut their churches down. I was determined not to become a statistic.

I know every pastor or leader starts out with a lot of excitement. They believe they are going to change the world. With this dream comes a faith that believes that "if God called me to do this supernatural work, He will provide everything I need for this journey." This is true. But every pastor eventually sees that His provision usually doesn't come the way they planned for it to come. The rubber band of our faith will always be stretched through our family, finances, and a fervent desire for self-fulfillment.

The purpose for your destruction is not only about stopping you

---

All ministry families are under constant attack. Ours was no exception. The joy that once consumed me in the early years of ministry began to turn to frustration and isolation. But, like a slow-developing poison in your body, it didn't happen overnight. Slowly but surely, depression was setting in. The Enemy was laying the groundwork for my destruction.

The thing you must understand is this: the purpose for your destruction is not only about stopping you. The Devil is bringing you down to stop what your vision will mean to hundreds, thousands, and even millions of other people.

All truly called men and women of God know their mandate is from heaven. We know our purpose is bigger than ourselves. But without fail, somewhere along the journey we are all tempted to turn our focus in another direction. We lose "sight" of our "first love."

Prayer, study, and a drive to "win the lost" fueled our heart in the beginning. Unfortunately, this inevitably turns to budgets, facilities, and a pursuit to just "pay the bills." It is in those times that the Enemy comes to us and disguises his voice to sound like God. We begin to convince ourselves that we need to change certain areas in our lives to "meet the greater good." Compromise replaces conviction and, eventually, leads to a life of contradiction.

I knew in my heart what the Lord had called me to do, but—like one of Scripture's most famous men of faith—I began to look for ways to help God fulfill His vision for me.

This is when ministry life becomes dangerous. We "think" we know what we saw. Buildings, television programs, books, schools, and church plants around the world is what we saw. God has a way of showing all of this to us in the initial stages, but He rarely shows us the journey to get there.

I needed God to hurry up and get this thing going. What was He waiting on? Had He forgotten all that I was supposed to do? I knew in my heart what the Lord had called me to do, but—like one of Scripture's most famous men of faith—I began to look for ways to help God fulfill His vision for me.

In my *waiting*, I decided to *wander* down an alternate road. It would lead to a make-or-break moment.

Doing God a Favor

Abram was a man of God. He was not perfect by any means, but he certainly had a strong relationship with God. This is evidenced by the fact that he had one-on-one verbal conversations with the Lord. I am pretty sure that didn't happen to most people!

Genesis 15 tells us of one of those conversations.

The Lord said to Abram, "Do not be afraid, Abram. I am your shield, your exceedingly great reward" (Genesis 15:1b).

The word *reward* in Hebrew is *sakar*. This word simply means, "payment of a contract."[2] From the very beginning of the conversation, God explained that He was all Abram would ever need to walk in His purpose and favor.

But the first words out of Abram's mouth were, "Lord, what will You give me…" He continued, "I am childless; therefore if You really want me to be fulfilled and have a legacy—give me a child." (Genesis 15:2, author's paraphrase).

It is the nature of man. God speaks to us and lets us know He is all we need. Then we convince ourselves that we need proof. If God is really going to be there for us through everything in life, He needs to show us a sign. This is where man has always messed up.

Adam walked with God daily, but it was not enough for him. Adam wanted to eat from God's tree. Moses was chosen by God to lead His people to freedom, but it wasn't enough for Him. He disobeyed God in the wilderness. God told him to speak to the rock, and fresh water would flow out of it. He struck the rock instead. He wanted the water to flow from the rock "his way."

David was a man after God's own heart. He was blessed with the greatest kingdom in history, but it wasn't enough for him. Instead of being happy that he had the most beautiful women in the world in his palace, he wanted the wife of another man. The list could go on and on.

2. Strong's Concordance, H7939, "*sakar*."

We hear God, and we believe God in the moment. We preach the vision and tell everyone what the Lord has said. But when it doesn't happen in our timing, we begin to quietly devise a plan to make it come to pass "our way."

In His compassion, God tells Abram that he will have a son. God tells Abram that this son will be his heir, and that He will give him the desires of his heart.

I am sure Abram thought his wife Sarai would conceive immediately. She did not. They tried again—nothing. Abram must have asked himself: What is happening here? Did I misunderstand God? Did He really mean what He said? Maybe we are supposed to do something to make it happen?

Something very interesting happens in Genesis 16. Sarai makes a proclamation toward the plan of God for their lives. What she says will not only change their journey, but also affect nations and ethnic groups for the entire future of mankind. Her words seemed to only affect their little household at the time, but she didn't realize that her words would set into motion war after war as well as the deaths of millions of people to come.

In her waiting she got impatient and decided to help God in His plan. She looked at her husband and suggested something that would be unthinkable in any of our homes. " See now, the Lord has restrained me from bearing children. Please, go in to my maid; perhaps I shall obtain children by her" (Genesis 16:2).

We need to break this down.

First, Sarai says, "The Lord has restrained me from bearing children." This should be the first sign we are on the wrong path. When anyone begins to believe or state that God didn't mean what He said, look out!

In Sarai's pain and lack of self-worth, she began to blame herself. Maybe she had done something wrong. She replayed the words of the prophecy over and over in her head.

Wait a minute, she thought, *God only said that Abram's son would come from his body. He didn't really specifically mention me. Maybe He wasn't talking about me at all. I will let Abram have sex with my servant, and I will make the child ours. This way, we can go ahead and start walking in the promise.*

When Abram heard his wife's proposal he was probably very shocked, but he did what she had suggested. He bought into the plan.

It looked like it worked. It looked like it was the will of God. Sarai's handmaiden, Hagar, immediately became pregnant with a son. They named him Ishmael. However, when Sarai looked into the eyes of a pregnant Hagar, she knew what she had done was wrong.

However, when Sarai looked into the eyes of a pregnant Hagar, she knew what she had done was wrong.

From an Old Hay Barn to the NFL

All my life I have loved sports. In fact, my dream was never to become a preacher. I wanted to be a coach. During my high school football days, I was always fired up. I was a motivator for my teammates. It was common to see me head-butting my fellow gladiators, just to whip them up into a frenzy. When I was on the sidelines, I would run up and down the fence, waving a towel and screaming at the crowd to get up and cheer for our team.

I look back now and realize the call on my life was trying to get out, but I didn't want to hear it.

I took my love for sports into my marriage and ministry. In fact, in the state of Alabama, it is a requirement! Instead of being a coach of athletes, I was now a coach of believers.

I had been in a lot of games, and I knew the feeling of fluctuating momentum. I had seen it go both ways. The direction of this shift in ministry was obvious. It was going down. When the finances of our church began to tumble, it directly affected every area of my life. I was the only paid staff in our little church.

When a church planter's offerings go down, he doesn't get paid. The expenses of the house of God come first. This meant that throughout the years of pastoring our church full-time, I had to find several side jobs to survive.

One such opportunity came in the form of a marketing company. Very quickly, I saw the potential of how this could help our home. I jumped in and learned all I could. Almost immediately, those in leadership saw my gift to motivate.

In a very brief time, I was filling hotel meeting rooms to capacity. In fact, within a couple of months I was speaking to more people in one setting than I had been speaking to in a month in my church. It felt good. No, it felt great! My sense of vision, and a desire to be appreciated, was being fulfilled. I felt like my gift was being acknowledged. My flesh was loving it.

To be completely transparent, I should add this: I was not really making much money at all, but I didn't care. I was having fun for the first time in a long time! The people who had helped me get started encouraged me to share a brief testimony about the Lord at the end. Occasionally, I would get a chance to pray for people. God was using me in the business world.

Not long after that, I was asked to travel to Montgomery, AL, to speak at a meeting. I didn't realize that one of the greatest athletes in the history of the University of Alabama would be in attendance. He was in the company, too, and was very successful.

I knocked it out of the park that night. One of my football heroes came up to me and asked me to start doing meetings for his family. Of course, I said yes. He was, and still is, a legend. This man was playing for the Dallas Cowboys at the time and had also played for the Green Bay Packers. I was star-struck.

We became friends and exchanged cell numbers. One day I received a call from him. He stated that he wanted to fly me to New Orleans to do a presentation for friends on the Saints football team. I was in awe. Shortly thereafter, I was flying all over the Southeast. Atlanta Falcons, New Orleans Saints, Tennessee Titans, Dallas Cowboys. The little hay barn church pastor was living large.

I had never felt more appreciated. I had never felt more fulfilled until I came home and preached to my little church in the country. Then I felt the opposite.

I didn't fully realize it at the time, but my heart was becoming divided. I had convinced myself that this new avenue was the will of God for my life. This must have been what God meant when He said I would speak to thousands. I had millionaires calling me on a weekly basis, asking me to talk to people for them. They would even say things like this to me: "Pastor Larry, you are the man. I appreciate you, brother."

But on Sundays I was speaking to less than fifty people. People who I was beginning to resent. "Why didn't they see what's on me? Why couldn't they appreciate what they had in me?" I was on a dangerous path. But I didn't see it that way. I was helping God out.

I didn't realize it, but I was slowly losing my vision. I could still see, but it was getting blurry. I was having double vision.

I didn't realize it, but I was slowly losing my vision. I could still see, but it was getting blurry. I was having double vision.

Competing Visions

So Abram had relations with Sarai's servant girl, Hagar. She immediately conceived, and the news was reported to the whole camp. Abram was to be a father!

How quickly things had changed. In Sarai's attempt to help God, she had removed herself from the promise. When she saw the look in Hagar's eyes, she knew what a mistake she had made. Sarai went immediately to her husband and confessed that she had missed God, but it seemed to be too late. Ishmael was on his way. The vision appeared to have been changed.

She continued, "My wrong be upon you! I gave my maid into your embrace; and when she saw that she had conceived, I became despised in her eyes. The Lord judge between you and me" (Genesis 16:5).

Abram replied, "Indeed your maid is in your hand; do to her as you please" (Genesis 16:6). In other words, "This is your mess; you fix it." Thanks a lot, Abram!

So Sarai dealt harshly with Hagar, and this caused her to leave the village. Hagar ran for her life and the life of her unborn son.

The truth is that Hagar was innocent. She hadn't asked for any of this. In Sarai's attempt to make sense of God's promise and help Him, she made a very poor decision. She decided to find fulfillment in the lives of others. But what Sarai didn't realize is that her decisions not only affected her life and her husband's life, but also Hagar's, Ishmael's, and the entire world.

We all do the same thing. God speaks a promise to us, and we praise Him for it. We walk in it. We tell everyone about it, but when it doesn't happen exactly the way we envisioned it we make our own path, not realizing that our decisions have lifelong repercussions.

When it doesn't happen exactly the way we envisioned it we make our own path, not realizing that our decisions have lifelong repercussions.

Abram was eighty-six years old when Ishmael was born. It would be another fourteen years before the true promise would be born (Isaac).

Abram was ninety-nine years old when God came to him and let him know his wife Sarai was pregnant. She was eighty-nine years old, and completely barren by this time.

It must have really seemed that God's will was Hagar. But God's Word tells us: "He who has begun a good work in you will complete it" (Philippians 1:6).

"The Lord is not slack concerning His promise, as some count slackness, but is longsuffering toward us" (2 Peter 3:9).

Those fourteen years seemed like an eternity, but God had never changed His mind. His vision was the same; it was Sarai's and Abram's that had changed.

When God told Abram that it was time for the true vision to be accomplished, He made some pretty substantial changes. They were name changes. Abram's name would now be Abraham, and his wife's would be Sarah. Their son would be named Isaac.

And this time, God made more than a promise. He also established a covenant. The Abrahamic covenant or blessing could never have belonged to Ishmael. The blessing was reserved for God's perfect will—

Isaac. It didn't take long for Sarah to realize that the two visions could not live together. Hagar and Ishmael had to go!

There is only room for one vision in your life. You can't live in harmony with God's will and your will at the same time. The plan of the Lord must be the only one in the camp.

You can't live in harmony with God's will and your will at the same time. The plan of the Lord must be the only one in the camp.

It is never easy to let "your will" be crucified. One of the hardest things in the world to do is break ties with your past mistakes. It is even harder to declare that they will never live with you again. This was a very painful time for Abraham. He loved Ishmael. He may have been a mistake, but he was his son.

But he had to go.

In my own life, I was quickly coming to a point where my Ishmael also had to go. Unfortunately, it would take a little more time to get my attention.

A False Sense of Success

If I were to ask you for your definition of success, I am sure I would have many different responses. One may say "being debt free," while another's definition may be "owning my own company" or "making my first million." You might even say "being a good parent" or "traveling the world and making a difference."

If you would have asked me for my definition of success during that season in my life, it would have been very different than it was in the beginning of our ministry. My vision had changed. I loved our church, and I certainly loved preaching the gospel, but I desired to be appreciated more than anything.

I know this was tied to being dropped and broken by two different fathers. I had lived my whole life trying to make at least one of the two men in my life to just be my father. I desired their approval and acceptance more than anything in this world. Neither came through. So I decided I was going to get that approval from the praises of others.

Not long after all the jet-setting of my business presentations around the NFL elite began, it all came crashing down. The company was shut down due to unscrupulous practices in the home office. I stayed in touch with my hero football friend from Alabama and the Dallas Cowboys. There were occasional calls from some of the other NFL players, but when the business folded, my purpose did, too.

Just like that, it was gone. I was back to the life of a country preacher: in a hay barn.

Then a business associate I had met through one of our NFL meetings called me. We discussed a new business venture that we would start ourselves. It was a field with which I was a little familiar because I had done this type of work in the past.

So we stepped out and launched our own business. The feelings I had from my previous business venture returned. I was excited. I was about to be a true success in life. This business was not going under. I knew the owners!

I owned fifty percent of my own company. I actually named our company. That alone made me feel like a success.

Our business grew quickly, and we realized we needed capital to grow to the next level. We searched and found some investors. They would invest money, and in return we gave them a small portion of the ownership of our company.

The workload grew extensively and began to take over my life. Gone were the days of flying to NFL camps. My days were now consumed with paperwork, phone calls, and cold-calling businesses. All of this while still pastoring full time. Not to mention the roles of father, husband, and even softball coach.

I was fading quickly. I was tired. I didn't feel fulfilled anymore. I didn't feel needed anymore. Truthfully, I didn't feel anything anymore. During this period of my life, there were a few pivotal moments. One of those days will never be forgotten.

Seconds Away from Breakdown

It was a Sunday morning before church. I was as physically, emotionally, and spiritually tired as I had ever been. I was in my little office on the back side of the hay barn, looking over my sermon for that day. I distinctly remember saying, "I don't want to go out there. I don't want to see those people. I am tired of all of this. I want out. I am done. I can't do this anymore."

It was at that moment that I leaned back in my chair and felt a darkness begin to descend upon me. It was so thick I could literally feel it on my skin. My head began to swirl, and my heart raced. I closed my eyes, and felt the darkness entering my skin and piercing into my being. It was real.

I had never felt anything like that in my life. Then I heard a very clear voice in my heart. It was a voice I had not heard that clearly in a long time. It was the voice of God. "Son, you are seconds away from a nervous breakdown, but I am warning you before it happens. You can get up, rebuke it, and stop it, or you can allow it to take over."

Thankfully, I jumped up and rebuked the Devil, and repented to God. I went out there that day and told my congregation what had just happened. They loved me, prayed for me, and let me know they were there for me. I knew change was coming, but I wasn't sure what it would be. I just knew I couldn't continue going in this direction.

I knew change was coming, but I wasn't sure what it would be. I just knew I couldn't continue going in this direction.

I couldn't just walk away from our company. This was not just a "job." Even after transferring ownership to our investors, I still owned over a third of the company. It was my baby. I had named it, remember?

So what was I going to do? How would anything be able to change? Was God telling me to resign from the church and pursue the business instead? I clearly was operating under two visions for my life. I needed God to do something to shake me. I needed clarity.

Will You Sacrifice What You Want?

Most people would have thought the tests were over now, but God needed to see if Abraham was "all in" with his faith. He was about to be asked to do the hardest thing any father could ever do. He had already endured the pain of having to put his firstborn son (Ishmael) out of the camp. He had watched the son he loved walk away in shame. But even though he loved him, he knew he was not the promise.

After many years of raising his true promise (Isaac), God suddenly came to Abraham with a very strange command.

"Take now your son, your only son Isaac, whom you love, and go to the land of Moriah, and offer him there as a burnt offering on one of the mountains of which I shall tell you" (Genesis 22:2).

Abraham rose early the next morning, got supplies and a team, and headed toward Moriah to do what the Lord had said. I realize this implies he had had no second thoughts and just did it, but this goes against human nature and certainly the heart of a father.

I can hear the thoughts of Abraham running through his head that night as he tried to sleep. *What? You tell me to send my firstborn away, and now you want me to kill the only son I have left? The one you said would be the promise?*

Nevertheless, he did what the Lord said to do.

The interesting thing is that when they got to the base of the mountain, Abraham made a statement that seemed to go against the command of God. He looked at his team of servants and said, "Stay here with the donkey; the lad and I will go yonder and worship, and we will come back to you" (Genesis 22:5).

We will come back to you! Was that a statement of rebellion or faith? Was Abraham stating that he was about to openly defy God to His face on the top of the mountain? Or could it be that Abraham had received a special revelation of who God really is?

Even though his faith had helped him make a bold statement at the base of the mountain, his flesh was scared at the top.

I believe Abraham had been through so much with God that he had gained an understanding of the nature of God. This revelation was not common to most Old Testament characters. Abraham got to "know" God. *He was God's friend.*

Could it be that he knew this moment was bigger than he was? That it was bigger than Isaac? Maybe he realized this was a dress rehearsal for the greatest day in history. Is it possible that Abraham had a supernatural revelation of the power of the resurrection?

As they climbed the mountain, Isaac said, "'Look, the fire and the wood, but where is the lamb for a burnt offering?' And Abraham said, 'My son, God will provide for Himself the lamb for a burnt offering'" (Genesis 22:7b–8).

This was a preview of the coming proclamation of John the Baptist. He would say of his cousin Jesus: "Behold! The Lamb of God who takes away the sin of the world!" (John 1:29b).

Even though his faith had helped him make a bold statement at the base of the mountain, his flesh was scared at the top. Can you imagine the emotion of a father as he bound his only son's hands and feet, and placed him on an altar of sacrifice?

But Isaac laid quietly as he watched his father raise the knife to kill him. Suddenly, in that moment, the Angel of the Lord proclaimed, "Do not lay your hand on the lad, or do anything to him; for now I know that you fear God, since you have not withheld your son, your only son, from Me" (Genesis 22:12).

Until we are prepared to give God everything we have, we have not given Him anything.

Notice that He said "your only son." Obviously, the sacrifice of Isaac was a type and shadow of what Jesus would do on the cross.

This was also a very bold statement regarding vision. The Angel of the Lord plainly called Isaac Abraham's "only son"! This meant, he was the only vision. God was making His plan clear: "The other (Ishmael) was your vision, Isaac is my vision, says the Lord!"

It's one thing to send something away and cut ties with the will of the flesh, but it is another thing to be willing to sacrifice what is closest to your heart. No one wants to kill what they've created. Our natural response would be, "God, I can't give You that. It's all I have." The Lord's response would be, "That's all I want: all you have."

Until we are prepared to give God everything we have, we have not given Him anything.

Remember, it's not your vision anyway. It is God's vision. That is why Abraham said to Isaac, "My son, God will provide for Himself the lamb for a burnt offering." Some translations say, "God will provide Himself a lamb." Jesus was, and is, the Lamb.

I know it doesn't make sense, but sometimes God has to take us on a journey, and He put us in difficult situations. He is not looking for us to "lose it all" or "sacrifice everything we own." He wants to know our heart. Are we willing to walk away from the things that satisfy our flesh? Are we willing to sacrifice our desires for His vision?

When you can look at true sacrifice as worship, you are positioned for greatness.

Abraham told his team at the base of the mountain that they were going to "worship." When you can look at true sacrifice as worship, you are positioned for greatness.

They came down the mountain with a story of deliverance for the ages.

I am sure the Enemy told him, "What a pathetic father you are. You are going to kill your own son!" But in that act of worship, God had found a friend. This seeming failure of a father would be known as Father Abraham to all generations. Father to the nations!

The Day a Biscuit Changed My World

Some of the greatest moves of God I have ever experienced took place in the old hay barn. I believe God honored the arduous work of the volunteers of our church who turned the barn into a nice place of worship. We were just a small group of dreamers who believed God had called us to change the world. Nothing was going to stop us. The Devil would never be able to hinder the vision that was within us.

I can remember walking out the back of the barn and just staring into the open field. I dreamt of building a large sanctuary, school, and Bible college right there in the cow pasture! I could literally see it. I believe that sometimes, I could even smell it! The same vision God had placed in me from day one was still there. It had never left me. I took it to every location. I simply believed God was going to do it.

That was the early days. After years of financial, personal, and mental struggle, I was at a point of no return. I somehow pushed through all my stress and near nervous breakdown and declared, "We are going to find a way to make our church grow!"

But the same problems remained in my life. I was being pulled in so many directions. Sandy and I began to feel a stirring inside of us for dramatic change. In my spirit, I knew the Lord was preparing us for another move. I didn't know when, and I didn't know how, but I knew the vision was not going to happen on that piece of property. During this season, Sandy and I drove in every direction for a twenty-mile radius. There was nothing available for purchase or even rent that would justify moving our small congregation.

Then one day, my wife called me with an urgent request.

"Larry, I know you are busy today. But could you meet me for breakfast? We can get us a biscuit and sit down and talk. I need to tell you something!"

I freaked out. Sandy never called and asked to meet for breakfast so that she could tell me something important! My mind was racing. I feared what I was about to hear.

When I arrived at the local restaurant, she was already seated. We ordered our breakfast and sat down. She went immediately to the purpose of her phone call. She began to weep. Then I really freaked out! *What is about to happen?* I wondered.

Sandy looked me in the eye and said, "Hear me out. Larry, I feel like God has told me that we are supposed to buy the Old Rock School in Pinson. That is our next building." My mouth dropped to the table. Let me explain.

The Old Rock School is located a little less than twenty miles from Birmingham, AL. It is in a city called Pinson. The settlement of Pinson is older than Birmingham. The school was built in 1921 by area residents.

The school took its name from the rocks that the local settlers handpicked and transported by horse and buggy to the location. Those rocks would become the exterior of the school. Thus, the name: Old Rock School. Sounds great, right? Not so much.

The once-beautiful structure was now abandoned and condemned. It had been vacant for almost ten years. Weeds and trash had taken over this icon of a building. The Old Rock School was a dump. Homeless people lived in it. Prostitution took place within its walls. Drug deals went down in the hallways that once were filled with students. And now my visionary wife wanted us to move our church there!

When we finished breakfast, she said, "Let's go break in. I think the back door is rotten, and has fallen in." So like any good husband, I said, "Of course, darling. Let's go."

We drove around the back of the building, and sure enough, there was no problem getting in. The entire door was gone, and the place was wide open to whoever would like to enter. As we stepped in, you could immediately smell the stench of urine, dead animals, and other things I will not list.

The back door entered the elevated stage portion of an old gymnasium. Half of the stage had collapsed and fallen to the ground. We almost fell in, too! When we looked down into the hole of what used to be a stage, there was an old upright piano lying on its side and decaying. It was just a microcosm of the rest of the building. The piano was once used for great things; now it was forgotten and left to rot.

For the first time in years,
I could see the vision clearly again.

The graffiti and drawings on the walls were the worst I had ever seen. The floor was littered with used needles, empty whiskey bottles, beer cans, and other "used stuff." The building had been condemned by the local authorities and was not fit to be used for anything. It was literally in ruins. Its destiny was further decay and, eventually, demolition.

But when we walked in the building, it came alive! My vision was restored. I could feel my spirit leaping within me. For the first time in years, I could see the vision clearly again. This was it. This is where it would happen. We walked through the entire complex. We explored hallways that were filled with trash and fallen pieces of ceiling and wood.

What were we thinking? Had we lost our mind? Nope—we had just seen the future!

Rebuild the Old Waste Places

One of my favorite verses is in Isaiah. It says, "Those from among you shall build the old waste places; you shall raise up the foundations of many generations; and you shall be called the Repairer of the Breach, the Restorer of Streets to Dwell In" (Isaiah 58:12).

As we walked through the dilapidated building that everyone else had given up on, we were restored. I saw my wife's eyes light up like I hadn't seen in a long time. I felt my whole perspective of ministry being rekindled. Who would have ever dreamed that walking through a building that was worthless would be the catalyst I needed to remind me of who I was?

When I say the building was in bad condition, you probably can't imagine how bad it really was. Only those who saw it then will ever begin to realize the amount of work that loomed before us. After several hours of walking through the building, taking pictures and video as we went, we sat down to talk about all we had just experienced.

The obvious question I had was, "How much do they want for it?" Sandy told me she had called about it, and I probably needed to sit down. She said the asking price was $1.8 million!

"What? Are you kidding me? We are barely running one hundred people right now. Most of them are youth and kids!" She said, "I know, but I think they are getting ready to reduce the price."

I called and sure enough, they had reduced it to $1.25 million! I quietly laughed when they told me that, but I responded very professionally to them: "OK, thank you so much. We will get back with you soon. We are very interested."

We met with our elders and discussed everything. They were in shock, but onboard. They were visionaries, too!

I remember laughing as someone said, "What's the maximum we will offer?" I replied, "How about we stop at a million?" Everyone laughed again. I continued, “Realistically, what’s the difference between a million and one hundred thousand? We don’t have either one! Let’s just have crazy faith, and believe!”

As the elders walked through the facility, you could see the concern on their faces. But honestly, it wasn’t the first time I had ever seen that on their countenances. We had already restored two buildings before this one. Rebuilding and restoring was what we did!

I will not go into the restoration process at this point. I will cover that a little later, but I will say that in my heart it was already restored. Most importantly to me, I was being restored.

The old waste places of my heart were being rebuilt as I walked through that building.

The old waste places of my heart were being rebuilt as I walked through that building. The foundations of many generations were being laid in Pinson, AL. We had been called to be “the repairers of the breach and the restorers of streets to dwell in.”

I Hear My Father Calling

We had no idea how we would secure the financing. We were considered as “high risk” as you could be in the eyes of a bank. We had good credit, but we were small and only had a small group of giving families. What we did have though was the favor of God!

For the first time in years, I was no longer thinking about how to get out of the ministry. I was now thinking about how to take our church to the next level.

Even so, there was still the issue of the business part of my life. At that time, I still owned thirty-seven percent of the company I had cofounded. I was also the “back office” guy. That meant I was handling most of the paperwork and follow-up from my home office.

After walking through the Old Rock School on another day, I felt the Lord tell me what I had to do. I drove home that day and laid it out before my wife. We were scheduled to have a corporate board meeting in Nashville, TN, that weekend. I would normally have driven to the meeting by myself, but I asked Sandy to go with me on this one. I was really struggling with what I felt I must do.

When we arrived, we sat in the car silently. I asked my wife to pray for me. I needed wisdom and I needed holy boldness. She prayed a very powerful prayer, and then she said, "I trust you. I'll be right here praying for you the whole time, baby."

As I entered the boardroom, I just sat down in my chair quietly. We all shared our hellos and discussed some outstanding business. At the conclusion of the meeting, I stood and read a prepared statement. I thanked all of them for being a part of such a great company and believing in our dream. I especially thanked our investors who had made it possible for us to expand.

I know God will bless whatever direction I go, but there is only one perfect will for my life. I have been called to preach the gospel to the world. I am a pastor.

Then I read the last paragraph of my statement. It went something like this: "I have enjoyed my time in the business world. It has given me great fulfillment. I have contemplated making this world my future. I know God will bless whatever direction I go, but there is only one perfect will for my life. I have been called to preach the gospel to the world. I am a pastor. I hear my Father calling. I must obey His voice. Therefore, tonight, I resign from the company. I am releasing all my shares of ownership in this company to the board of directors to distribute them as you see fit. I know I could step back from the workload of the company, and receive royalties from my ownership, but I feel that I must rely totally on God and the ministry He has called me to do. Thank you for everything. I am going back home to get busy building our ministry."

I walked back to the car and met Sandy. She immediately said, "Well, how'd it go?" My simple response was, "I hear my Father calling."

I See Greatness In You

The same girl who saw greatness in me outside of the courthouse in chapter one looked at me and said, “I’m proud of you. Now let’s go home and get ready for the next building and the next level.”

Chapter Seven

Favor Is Better Than Money

You Have to Let Them Go

As you have learned in the earlier chapters of this book, I have major father issues.

The man I grew up with and thought was my father was not actually my biological father. He physically and emotionally abused me for most of my childhood. The psychological effects of those years are still with me today. At times, I still battle some of the same issues from when I was a kid.

Later in my young life, I found out he was not my father. My real dad was out there somewhere, and I was determined to find him. I did find him, and he seemed to be the father I always wanted. Sadly, it didn't work out with him either. He was only in my life for a brief moment, and then it was over.

Now I was a grown man. I was married and had two young daughters. I found myself reading books on how to be a good dad. I watched other fathers and learned from them. Simply put, I had no clue what a father looked like. I remember attending a large men's conference in Birmingham with one of the most widely known preachers at that time. I had taken a few of the men from our church with me. It was powerful.

On the last night of the conference, the speaker asked for all the pastors to come down and stand in front of the stage. I quickly ran to the altar. I loved this preacher, and I wanted to get close to him. I admired him greatly and wanted whatever mantle of anointing that was on him to get on me.

As I stood there, he walked straight towards me. This tower of a man stood about three feet from me and pointed his finger into my chest. He was still looking at the massive crowd, but his finger was pointing at me! These were his words: "You have been asked to be a father to many, and you have said, 'Lord, how can I be a father to many, when I don't even know what a father is?'"

I cried out and fell to the floor. I had said those words so many times, they could never be counted. I wept so hard my body shook. "How, Lord, am I supposed to be a good father to my children, and a spiritual father to those in my life? I have no clue how to do it."

I heard the Lord say, "Son, you have to let them go! You have to forgive them." I thought that I had let it go, but realized I had not.

I said to God, "I forgive both of my fathers for all they have done. I know down deep in their heart, they loved me. I know they just didn't know how to be my father. I will not be defined by them, and I will not hold a grudge towards them. I do not hate them. I love them and want them to have a great life. If they want to be in my life, they can. If they don't, they don't have to be. I release them, and I forgive them."

I stood up, and I knew I was free!

A Father to the Fatherless

Psalm 68:5 says the Lord is a "father to the fatherless," and He truly is.

I had no Father but God.

I look back over the years, and I see the love of my heavenly Father operating throughout my life. He manifested Himself in other men along the journey: uncles, men of God in my church, and certainly my grandfather. These men were not perfect. In fact, some of them were not even Christians. But God used them to father me.

My mother did everything she could to be everything I needed in my life. It was impossible for her to be my father, but she tried. In many ways, she succeeded. For years, I gave her Father's Day cards because she was the only father I thought I would ever have.

But all of them were not enough for where I was going. I needed a man of God to be a spiritual covering for me in my life. I was a pastor, but I didn't have a pastor.

But more than anything, I wanted a father. My life was changed forever when I realized that God had finally sent me a pastor, friend, and father.

I needed a man of God to be a spiritual covering for me in my life. I was a pastor, but I didn't have a pastor.

I have purposely avoided naming anyone in my book. I have not even named my two fathers, my mother, my brother or anyone else. I have only named my wife. My reason for this is simple. I have no desire to defame or destroy anyone personally, or their families. I know that I have said some hard things regarding my fathers, but they are one hundred percent true. Trust me, I could have gone further, but this was never my intention. This story is a story of redemption, forgiveness and greatness—not a story of condemnation.

That being said, I will name one other person. He is the man that God sent into my life to show me what a father looks like. He couldn't have come into my life at a more perfect moment. This man has given me guidance in family, marriage, finances, ministry, and manhood. His name is Frankie Powell.

Pastor Frankie is my father. He is proud of me and affirms me. He has never abandoned me. He has walked with me through some of the toughest moments in my life. You may never know him, but I hope you get the chance to meet him. I just wanted to take a moment in my first book to acknowledge him. I don't believe I would be sitting here writing about my life without him "being in my life."

A Man That Was Full

In Acts 6, the early church was exploding. Pentecost power was still fresh on each of them. The disciples were doing all they could humanly do. They were preaching, teaching, praying for the sick, taking care of the widows and orphans, and facilitating the foundations of the early church. They were so busy with all the "duties" of the ministry that the widows were not receiving the care they had been receiving in the past.

As a result of this, people began to murmur and complain. Imagine that, church people complaining…but I digress. The disciples realized they had to do something, so they summoned the multitude of believers together and released the plan to continue their growth and effectiveness. They chose seven men from the leadership of the early church. Each one had to have a good reputation and be full of the Holy Spirit and wisdom. Among the seven was a man named Stephen.

His story is short, but it's one of the most profound in the history of the church. Many believe the events that were about to happen in his life would be the catalyst for the massive explosion of the church, which would eventually reach the entire world.

Stephen preached with power. Miracles happened wherever he went. He was quickly promoted as one of the top "enemies" of the anti-Jesus religious crowd. But that did not stop him. I think it actually fueled him. Not because he desired vengeance or wished to embarrass the priests, but because he was full of love for them.

In fact, the interesting thing about Stephen is that he was so "full" of power, grace, and faith that those three words became a part of his name in the early church. Any time Stephen's name is ever mentioned in Scripture, it is accompanied by "full of…" It would either be "full of … power, grace, faith" or "the Holy Spirit." Incredible! He was so full of these things that those who knew him always acknowledged that he walked in these things whenever they mentioned his name.

Of course, if you know the story, this would ultimately lead to his death. Stephen was the first Christian martyr. He was stoned to death simply for preaching the gospel. Their hatred towards him was purely demonic. As he began to preach, they became so enraged that they engulfed him, biting him all over his body. But Stephen (full of…), just kept smiling and giving God praise. He had such a relationship with God that this moment caused the spiritual realm to be opened up to his natural eyes. Listen to how the Word describes it:

"But he [Stephen], being full of the Holy Spirit, gazed into heaven and saw the glory of God, and Jesus standing at the right hand of God, and said, 'Look! I see the heavens opened and the Son of Man standing at the right hand of God!'" (Acts 7:55–56, insertion mine).

Can you imagine a man's faith so strong that it caused Jesus to give them a standing ovation? The Bible tells us that Jesus is seated at the right hand of God the Father, but in this instance, He stood up for Stephen! What could have caused Jesus to open the windows of heaven and allow Stephen to peer into His glory, actually seeing his Savior standing on his behalf? Stephen was "full of" forgiveness!

Forgiveness is a very powerful emotion. It has the power to break any chain and give you peace in any situation. I want you to listen to how the Bible describes the horrible (and glorious) ending of the life of Stephen.

Forgiveness is a very powerful emotion. It has the power to break any chain and give you peace in any situation.

"Then they cried out with a loud voice, stopped their ears, and ran at him with one accord; and they cast him out of the city and stoned him. And the witnesses laid down their clothes at the feet of a young man named Saul. And they stoned Stephen as he was calling on God and saying, 'Lord Jesus, receive my spirit.' Then he knelt down and cried out with a loud voice, 'Lord, do not charge them with this sin.' And when he had said this, he fell asleep" (Acts 7:57–60).

His death was a major event in the early church.

When the men who stoned him took off their coats, they handed them to a young man named Saul. This was Saul of Tarsus, who would later become the apostle Paul. He stood and watched an innocent man be killed—just for being full of faith, love, grace, mercy, and forgiveness!

His final words seem very familiar. "Lord Jesus, receive my spirit … Lord, do not charge them with this sin." When he said these words—he fell asleep.

Stephen was full of Jesus' spirit. He was full of the love of Jesus. He was full of the grace of Jesus.

Look at the words of our Savior on the cross just before His death. "Then Jesus said, 'Father, forgive them, for they do not know what they do … And when Jesus had cried out with a loud voice, He said, 'Father, "into Your hands I commit My spirit.'" Having said this, He breathed His last" (Luke 23:34, 46).

Stephen was the embodiment of a Christ-follower. He realized the power of forgiveness.

It was that display of forgiveness that began to convict the heart of a bitter religious man named Saul. The memory of Stephen's display of Jesus would later come back to him on the road to Damascus. This is when Saul would meet the Messiah Himself.

Will You Forgive Me?

The power of forgiveness cannot be measured. It has the ability to save a marriage, heal a family, and even break generational curses.

On its own, it seems like a straightforward process. "I was wrong; will you forgive me?" But those seven words are some of the hardest a person will ever have to say. It goes against human nature.

As hard as it is to forgive, we must do it. There comes a time when we have to choose to move forward. And you can't move forward with unresolved unforgiveness.

You can't move forward with unresolved unforgiveness.

I was a perfect example of this. I was now married and a father to two small girls. I had already owned two businesses and was a full-time pastor of a small, but growing, church. Even so, I always felt like something was holding me back from going to the next level in my life and ministry. Down deep inside, I knew what it was.

Resentment.

I had said the words, "I forgive them (my two dads)," but I had never really let the resentment go. One day, I told God, "If I ever see either one of them again, help me to walk in total forgiveness." As I said in an earlier chapter, "Be careful what you wish for." Not long after that commitment to God, I ran into my first father, the man who had abused me physically and emotionally. I had not seen him in several years.

I was going in a door and he was coming out. You know, when I think about that now, it seems fitting. We were both shocked when we saw each other. I was the first to speak. "Hey Dad, how are you?" I don't know what I expected him to say at that moment, but I remember feeling let down when he just said, "I'm fine. How are you?" And then he kept walking to his car. That was it.

Suddenly I felt my spirit rise within me. I heard a voice inside me say, "This may be your last chance to be totally free. You know what you have to do."

Just before he got in his car, I yelled, "Hey, Dad, can I ask you a question?"

"Yes, what is it?" he replied. For a few seconds, I froze. I realized at that moment that I could have ripped him to shreds. I was not the little boy he mentally controlled anymore. I was a grown man. The Devil immediately tempted me to bust him, but I didn't.

"What is it?" he said again. I looked at the man that I had hoped would apologize to me my whole life, and I expected him to break down emotionally in that moment. But it didn't happen.

Instead, without another thought I blurted out, "If I've ever done anything to hurt you, will you please forgive me?"

My flesh immediately told me, *Ha, you got him. You just set him up. He knows you have never done one thing bad to him. He knows what he did to you. He is going to say, No son, I'm the one that needs to apologize to you.* I was ready to hear it. With his body halfway in the car, he said, "OK, I forgive you." He got in the car and shut the door. I was shell-shocked. I couldn't believe it.

But something amazing happened. Standing there on the outside of that door, I felt total freedom. It was over. There was nothing but love and total forgiveness in my heart for him. I was free. Wow, it felt incredible.

Then, just as I turned the doorknob to go in, I heard his car door open. He got out and said, "Larry, will you forgive *me* for what I've done?" Surprisingly, there were no tears. There were no feelings of justification. I was full of the joy of the Lord. I simply replied, "Dad, I already have. There's nothing to forgive. But thank you for asking." He shut the door and drove off.

To my knowledge, this would be the last conversation I would ever have with him.

Favor Is Better Than Money

I have followed a consistent pattern. I have shared my life's stories followed by biblical accounts of God's grace, mercy, restoration, forgiveness, and love in the lives of some of the more widely known characters in the Bible. I want to take a moment and veer in a slightly different direction for this chapter of the book.

Instead of talking about one character or story, I would like to talk about a subject. Favor.

One of the most famous preaching statements in the world is, "Favor is better than money!" It is a great shouting line, but it is also true. Favor truly is better than money.

Money can buy you a house, but it can't buy you a home. Money can buy you a bed, but it can't buy you a good night's sleep. Money can buy you a position or a title, but it can't buy you respect. You get the picture.

The favor of God can open doors that no man can shut. Favor can move the hearts of decision-makers on your behalf. Favor is not tied to what you deserve, or what you have earned. It is the decision of God. God decides who He blesses with His favor. It can never be earned.

Favor is not tied to what you deserve,
or what you have earned.
It is the decision of God.

Favor is not reserved for the religious elite or the longtime Christian. I've seen the undeniable favor of God on a brand-new believer who was just instantly delivered from addiction.

I've said it like this for years: "Favor ain't fair!"

I believe the favor of God was released into my life on another level when I totally forgave my father. I didn't just forgive my first father; I forgave my biological father that day as well. I never got the chance to ask my second father for my forgiveness. I lost contact with him and didn't know how to find him, but in my heart, I released both of them that day.

Honestly, I didn't know what favor was. I just began to walk in it. I was going to need it more than ever to help me through the journey that was about to unfold in our lives. We were about to move into a season of events that, to this day, is hard for me to believe really happened. If I didn't live them myself, I don't know if I would believe they were true.

The Old Rock School

We had walked through the Old Rock School many times and dreamed of having it for our next facility. It seemed impossible. They were still asking over one million dollars for a piece of property that was condemned as unusable. The value of the property was based on the land, not the buildings. Many years earlier, the county school board had voted to tear the buildings down and use the land for some other reason. The buildings were old and too small for the growing number of kids in our local city.

But the Old Rock School was an icon in our community and the local residents rose up and protested its demolition. They put signs everywhere that said: "Save Old Rock School" and "Don't Tear Down Our History."

Under the mounting public relations nightmare, the school board relented. They voted to not tear the buildings down, but they also decided to leave them standing and never do maintenance on them again.

The only thing vision needs
to succeed is favor.

So the Old Rock School sat vacant. Year after year, the elements took their toll. What was once a beacon of learning was now an eyesore in the heart of the city—but we had a vision for that old building. No one else could see it, but we saw it. That is what vision does. It allows you to see what no one else can see. The only thing vision needs to succeed is favor. We were walking in both.

Suddenly

Throughout Scripture we see instances of God showing up suddenly and unexpectedly. I have found the greatest miracles of deliverance or intervention happen in the least likely moments.

After the resurrection of Jesus, He told them to go into the city and pray together. He said, "Don't leave until you receive the promise of the Father. Holy power is coming, and you are going to change the world" (Acts 1:4, my paraphrase).

There were hundreds, if not thousands, who heard that command; but by the time we get to Acts 2 (only a few days later), the number had dwindled to 120. But they were a dedicated group. They were determined to see what the Lord had promised. They prayed and began to confess "unity." At some point, they realized, "We are in this together. We have to trust that Jesus will do exactly what He said He would do." So they prayed for the promise and they prayed in agreement. We don't know the exact minute, or even hour, when it happened, but Scripture clearly states: it happened quickly and unexpectedly.

"And suddenly there came a sound from heaven, as of a rushing mighty wind, and it filled the whole house where they were sitting. Then there appeared to them divided tongues, as of fire, and one sat upon each of them. And they were all filled with the Holy Spirit and began to speak with other tongues, as the Spirit gave them utterance" (Acts 2:2–4).

Suddenly, God filled the Upper Room with His Spirit.

It caught them all off guard, but they all responded the same way. They prayed and rejoiced. God did what He said He would do. He did it when He decided to do it. He didn't need the permission of man. He can show up whenever He wants to show up.

It is in the nature of God to "show up" in the most unexpected places and times. Why? Because He will not share His glory with anyone, anything, or any process. If you can make it happen on your own, then it was not a God-given vision.

Just think of the times that God showed up in the most unexpected and unlikely places.

For David, when he stood before a giant; for Daniel in the lion's den; when the rain fell in the time of Noah; as He spoke through the burning bush to Moses; at the tomb of Lazarus.

God specializes in the unexpected and the unlikely. He loves to hear people say, "How did that happen? It must be a miracle!"

I want to encourage you that God has an unexpected miracle for you. He is actively planning to show up and blow your mind. He needs you to stay in the game. Don't give up. Keep dreaming. Keep pushing. When you least expect it, *suddenly*, His favor will show up.

God has an unexpected miracle for you. He is actively planning to show up and blow your mind.

So Crazy It Just Might Work

The power of favor in your life cannot be taken lightly. If you are going to do something great for God, you are going to need favor. You will need favor with men, and favor with God.

Our church had never had a lawyer, accountant, financial expert, or anyone to advise us in anything we had ever done. So how in the world were we going to negotiate with the largest school system in our state for one of their pieces of property? Favor!

I needed God to suddenly give me a creative idea. I knew there was no bank in America that would even agree to talk to us, let alone lend us the money. How was this going to happen? I had no idea. I just had faith.

After several conversations on the phone, we had negotiated a price under one million. It might as well have been 100 million. We didn't have anything, except God!

So we prayed for favor. I specifically prayed for a God-inspired creative idea.

One night, "suddenly," it happened. I jumped up and began to type. God gave me a "favored" idea. It was crazy. It was unthinkable. Honestly, in the natural realm, it didn't have a chance. But, at that moment, I was full of faith.

God gave us the idea to tell the school board that we were their only shot! No one was ever going to buy these buildings. They were useless.

The "for sale" signs had been on them for ten years. It was a "hot potato." On the one hand, the land was extremely valuable to many businesses. On the other hand, no business would ever buy it. There were too many liabilities involved. They would have to tear the buildings down. The community would never allow that. So we were their only shot!

We told them we didn't want the land. We wanted the buildings. No bank would ever loan us the money to buy only seven acres of land, so here was God's creative idea:

We proposed they would give us the buildings, free of any type of payment for two years. This would give us the time to restore portions of the buildings to be used as collateral in a loan. That was not too outlandish.

The crazy faith proposal was the last line. "If we do not secure a loan to purchase the property within exactly two years from the signing date of the contract, we will vacate the building and leave all furnishing and improvements. We will return the buildings to you to sell for a greater profit."

We sent this letter of proposal, along with pictures of the state of vandalism and decay to the board. We waited for a response.

I remember telling our elders, "This is so crazy that it just might work."

After several weeks of waiting, we received a package in the mail from the board. I was shaking when I opened it. I believed in my heart that the vision for our church was tied to their response. I had totally given it to God.

I had walked away from my own company for this moment. I had put aside all the pain of my past, and forgiven all those who ever hurt me, for this moment.

We opened the letter and it simply said, "We agree to your terms."

Favor is better than money!

Sleep on It

We signed the contract and got to work. The place was so run-down that it took us two straight weeks just to get the trash out of the buildings. It took us another two weeks to clear the weeds and debris from around the exterior. I could take an entire chapter to describe all the memories made while working on those buildings. But for time purposes, I will simply say it was an incredible experience.

Imagine a church body of fewer than one hundred people working for fourteen months to restore a million-dollar project. Many volunteers worked six days a week on the property. Several came straight from work and labored through the night. Then they would get up and go to work again the next day.

It was one hundred percent volunteer labor. We only paid for a few minor jobs. Most everything was done for free. We had contractors who donated labor and materials.

One man, who lived two hours away, bought a camper and parked it in the back of the building for his workers to sleep in at night. He so believed in what we were doing that he put all his jobs on hold until we were done. He did all the plumbing and HVAC for free. He is one of the greatest men of God I know.

Fourteen months of work had transformed the old gymnasium into our sanctuary. The boys' and girls' locker rooms were now our restrooms. The decrepit classrooms of the past were now our nursery and children's classrooms. It was truly incredible.

We moved in and started having services fifteen months after signing a twenty-four-month lease. We had nine months to secure the financing. We had meetings with bank after bank, and everyone basically laughed in our faces. I believe we had been rejected, in some form, by eleven banks in seven months.

Then, "suddenly," someone told us about a small bank from another state that had just opened an office in Birmingham to service commercial loans. I called them and planned a meeting.

The loan officer was a young man who I could immediately tell was different from all the others. He genuinely wanted to know our story. He wanted to hear our vision. He was a believer, and he was excited about what God was doing in our church.

He said, "I'm going to bat for you. I'll do my best. I am making no promises, but I am going to try and make this happen." Well, that was all I needed to hear. I believed it was done.

In that season of my life, nothing was impossible. I simply didn't think there was any way it was not going to happen. After a couple of weeks, we received a call from the bank. They were optimistic that they could make something happen. We thought that meant they were ready to close.

Nothing could have been further from the truth. Because we were such a significant risk, we jumped through hoop after hoop. My faith was truly being tested. We were running out of time. I knew the exact ending date of the contract with the school board. Doomsday fell on a Friday.

We came to the last week of the two-year lease, and we still didn't have a closing or even the official letter of intent for the loan. The bank continued to assure me: It was going to happen. I had no other choice but to believe God.

Two days before the end of our lease, our loan officer called me. I remember it like it was yesterday. It was a Wednesday afternoon around 4:00 p.m. When I saw the number on my caller ID, my heart sank. I walked outside and sat down on a concrete block in the back of the old gymnasium (which was now our sanctuary). I sat alone.

The voice on the other end of the phone said, "Larry, I'm sorry." I was silent. My head fell to the ground. Every nerve in my body began to shake. I thought to myself, *No, I refuse to hear this.*

He continued, "Larry, I truly am sorry. I did everything I could. The board of our bank just contacted me, and said it is simply too risky. We can't do the loan." I could hear the pain in his voice. He was hurting, too. I responded, "Thanks, man. I really appreciate all you have done. It is in God's hands now." Then I hung up the phone.

I sat there on that block and cried. The pressure of fourteen months of work, six days a week, pushed down on me. I had told my church that God had spoken to me, that He was going to do it for us. How could I face them? What would I tell our elders? I wanted to get in my truck and drive to another state.

Then I remembered it was Wednesday. I had to teach in a couple of hours. My lesson that night was "The Favor of God." How in the world was I going to teach on that subject, when it appeared God had not come through?

"Suddenly," a strength entered my spirit. I stood up and began to praise God. I started walking around the back of that building, rebuking the Devil and quoting Scriptures about the favor of God. I cried out, "Favor is better than money. Favor is better than money. God, You don't need a bank. You are the bank!"

"Favor is better than money. God, You don't need a bank. You are the bank!"

I cleaned myself up, walked on that stage, and preached like a wild man. I preached about favor. I preached about who our source is. I preached about our vision.

When the service was over, I had a brief meeting with our elders to tell them what had happened. I will never forget the way one of them looked at me and said, "It is OK, pastor. We've done all we can do. Let's go home and sleep on it, and see what happens."

Now, I would be lying if I told you I slept like a baby that night. I didn't. But my faith was still strong.

Last-Second Favor

We woke up the next morning and expected a miracle. Nothing happened. No phone calls, no letters in the mail. Only the words, "Larry, I'm so sorry," ringing in my head.

All I could think about was that I had less than forty-eight hours to tell our congregation that we were a church without a building. We had nowhere to go. In over two years, we had raised and spent many thousands of dollars for the restoration process. All that money was down the drain. It looked like it was over.

When Sandy and I finally got up and got moving that day, we headed to Birmingham for some errands. Of course, the conversation was consumed with what we were facing. You could feel our faith dwindling with every mile we drove on the highway that day.

But then something stunning happened. I noticed that I had missed a call on my phone, and I had a voicemail. I pulled off the road and into a fast food joint parking lot. I put the voicemail on speakerphone so we could both hear it. The voice on the message was the voice of our loan officer.

He was filled with excitement. He said, "Larry, I don't know what to say. I can't believe this. This has never happened. I have never heard of this happening. I'm just going to read the e-mail to you that I received this morning."

We both sat silently, looking at each other, with our mouths wide open and our eyes about to pop out of our heads. What was he about to say?

It was a message from the president of the bank. We found out that he was a strong believer in Christ. He went back and read our vision for the building, and he decided to personally appeal to the board one more time on our behalf. He knew it was unprecedented to ask the board to reconsider a decision they had made earlier that same day. But, he felt "compelled" to try again for us. We had never met this man, and to this day I have no idea what his name is.

Our loan officer read the e-mail: "After reading the church's proposal, once again I felt I needed to approach our board on their behalf. I personally told them that I believed their church would be a good fit for us and would faithfully pay the loan. After discussion, the board decided to reverse their decision. Please inform the church we have agreed to finance the loan."

We began to scream at the top of our lungs. God had done it! He had really done it.

Favor is better than money. All the money in the world could not have moved on the heart of the president of a bank. God moved on his heart.

That Sunday, I told the whole story to our congregation. I told them about Wednesday, and I told them about Thursday. We had church! I've got a feeling some of you may be living in a Wednesday moment too, but I want you to know that there is a Thursday moment coming! Stand up, praise God, and rebuke the Devil. Begin to proclaim that "favor is better than money, favor is better than money. God, You are the bank! God, You are my Provider! I will not give up. You have called me to greatness."

Dedication Day

One of the greatest days in our ministry was the day we dedicated our building to the Lord. It was a day of worship and celebration, as well as an acknowledgment of all the demanding work that had brought us to that day. Fourteen months of blood, sweat and tears. Six months of rejection from bank after bank. Being told you had lost the building, only to find out you had gained the building all in one forty-eight-hour period. Wow! It was an incredible journey of faith and favor.

The dedication of our people had affected our community. Pastors from other churches sent their congratulations and support. People from other congregations joined us to celebrate a great day in the kingdom. The mayor of our city and all of the city council were present to recognize our church. It was filled with dignitaries. But the guest of honor was a young man who had gone into battle for us, a man who believed in us and took a chance on a bunch of dreamers from a hay barn: our loan officer.

We presented him with a plaque that bore the words of our appreciation. When I handed it to him, I asked him if he would share a few words. He accepted.

"I've never seen or heard of anything happening like this in my life. I've asked my colleagues who have been doing this a long time, and neither have they. I know that it can only be God. Who has ever heard of a bank changing their mind 'after hours,' on the same day of their rejection? I thank God I was a part of this. I am thankful I got to be a small part of what God is doing here." He said this with tears streaming down his face. We were all crying with him.

The news media was there to cover this amazing story. All the print media of Birmingham and the surrounding cities wrote articles promoting what God had done. Birmingham's local television stations interviewed me and others from the church and told our story to the masses. The Old Rock School was now Solid Rock Church. It had been saved from demolition. We had been saved from embarrassment. I had been saved from depression. It seemed like we were at the pinnacle of success. It was a long way from an old hay barn to this moment. What could possibly top this?

Little did we know, but our journey had just begun. God had bigger things for us, and greater challenges. Our faith would be tested over and over. I never felt closer to our vision than in that season of my life. I believed I would never come down from the high of that moment.

Little did I know that my world was about to come crashing down. In that building, I would face the darkest moments of my adult life. I felt like I had it all, but it wouldn't take long before I almost lost it all.

Chapter Eight

The Greatest Worst Day

The Slow Fade

Momentum is an amazing thing. Incredibly, some people don't think it even exists. They say, "It is all just in your head. It is not really a thing." Oh, but it is a very real thing.

Most of us have seen it play out in various sporting events. It looks like there is no hope for your team to come back and win the game. The announcers are already calling the game over. Then, when no one expects it—a blocked punt or an onside kick. The fans are stunned, and the opposing players are caught off guard. You can literally feel the atmosphere shift. Hope comes rushing in. Minutes earlier, you were calling for the coach to be fired; now, you are screaming that he is the greatest coach ever. You may still lose the game, but at that moment, you believe you have a chance.

This type of momentum is what I like to call "mythical momentum." It is only real to you because you can feel it. You are not even in the game, but it makes you feel like you are. You now believe you can *will* your team to victory.

Momentum is a powerful feeling,
but it can also be deceiving.

But the truth is, the players on the field are not being moved by momentum. They are focusing on the next play. They are trying to stick to the game plan and simply win the game. Momentum is a powerful feeling, but it can also be deceiving.

There is a very real definition of momentum, and it is not "mythical" or even sports related. It is physics. The online dictionary defines "momentum" as "the amount of motion occurring in something that is moving, or the force that drives something forward to keep it moving."[3]

When an object has momentum, it means it has been rolling or moving. It has been picking up speed. If it is moving, it feels amazing. You literally feel like there is nothing that can stop you, but eventually momentum always shifts—or comes to a screeching halt.

We had just come through fourteen months of momentum. Remodeling the Old Rock School had been a lot of demanding work, but it was momentum work! We were all driven; we had purpose. There was a goal that we were all working towards, and nothing was going to stop us. The truth is, nothing could stop us. What was in our heart to do, we did.

Just like in a big game, momentum can swing quickly and propel you to a win. Many times, it is a game that no one expected you to win; but you must always be careful of the dreaded "letdown." Oftentimes, we see teams that win games from momentum go on to lose the next week to a team they should have easily beaten.

The moments after a huge victory are the most dangerous moments. This is the seedbed for pride, arrogance, and entitlement.

If you are not watchful over your emotions, you will begin to read your own press clippings. Spiritual momentum is often the result of riding the high of the favor of God. If we do not stay focused on what was causing us to roll and pick up speed in the first place, we will find ourselves rapidly going in the opposite direction. This is a result of

3. "Momentum," *YourDictionary*, accessed January 27, 2018, http://www.yourdictionary.com/momentum.

living in the victories of the past and not continuing to do whatever you need to do for the momentum of your life to continue.

The moments after a huge victory are the most dangerous moments. This is the seedbed for pride, arrogance, and entitlement. It is very difficult, but this is the season in which you must stay the most focused on why you do what you do!

We had just come through one of the most miraculous, last-minute, miracles of provision that I had ever encountered. Our church had just saved a decrepit building from collapse and was now enjoying the fruit of our labors. The little country church from the "old hay barn" had finally made it. We were growing. First-time visitors were coming every Sunday. From the outside, it looked like explosive growth was about to be released.

But behind the scenes, I was going through a "slow fade." I was not aware of what was happening. I had worked so hard for so long that I decided it was time to sit down and rest a little. Well, that rest turned into laziness and, eventually, apathy. My body and my mind began to move into shutdown mode. My eating habits were horrible, and all my energy left me. I started having heart palpitations. I was in bad shape, but I allowed myself to be blind to it all. I was convinced that everything was OK.

Behind the scenes, I was going through a "slow fade." I was not aware of what was happening.

God was about to use a series of events to shake my world to the core. It would be a moment when I almost quit everything (for real). I was moving into a new season in which I would almost die physically. Honestly, I should have died. It was horrible, but it would prove to be lifesaving.

The Shepherd Who Lost His Way

We discussed David earlier, but I want to dig a little deeper into his story now. There are lessons from the life of this king that parallel many of our lives. The story of King David is one of the most amazing stories in human history. He is known all over the world for the famous battle scene between him and Goliath. But the story of David is so much more.

It is a tale of a young boy who miraculously rises from obscurity to become the most famous man in the known world. He would win epic battles and defeat enemies who outnumbered him tenfold. This same man would go on to make decisions that make us scratch our heads and wonder: how he could have been so careless?

David was human. Humans can do remarkable things, but we can also do very stupid things.

Many of our mistakes come after great successes. We begin to read our own headlines. Nowadays, they come in the form of tweets and social media posts. When you do something great, people immediately post their praise for you on a platform that is instantly worldwide.

King David was a remarkable man. He left such an impact on his world. Consider this: Israel has a star on their flag. That star is called the Star of David. Their national capital (Jerusalem) was established by David. Jerusalem is also known as the City of David. His story is incredible.

David didn't start in the palace. David's story began in isolation. It began in the wilderness. He was trained by his father to take care of their flocks. From a small child, he flowed in his purpose. He was a natural. David was a born shepherd!

By the time God sent the prophet Samuel to the house of Jesse, David's father, David was already taking care of the sheep by himself. He was only a young teenager, but he was a seasoned protector and provider of the sheep! The prophet Samuel was on a mission from God. He had been sent to anoint the next king. All the sons were lined up from the oldest to the youngest—except for David.

When it was time to anoint the king, Samuel went directly to the oldest. He was the obvious choice. The elder son would always receive the blessing. Eliab stood before Samuel, waiting to hear the life-changing words he would receive from the man of God. Samuel even said himself, "Surely the Lord's anointed is before Him!"

"But the Lord said to Samuel, 'Do not look at his appearance or at his physical stature, because I have refused him. For the Lord does not see as man sees; for man looks at the outward appearance, but the Lord looks at the heart'" (1 Samuel 16:6–7).

God made it very clear to the prophet why he was sending him to the house of Jesse. He was to only anoint the young man that was confirmed by God Himself. The Lord knew exactly who it would be, even if Samuel did not.

One by one, the sons came before Samuel in order of their age. Each one received the same words from God: "This is not him!" After all the sons had passed before him, Samuel asked, "Are these all your sons?" Jesse answered, "There remains yet the youngest, and there he is, keeping the sheep" (1 Samuel 16:11).

"There he is, keeping the sheep." Those words were the validation for the reason Samuel was there. God has always chosen to use those who keep the sheep. He is not just looking for kings. He is looking for shepherd-kings.

David was anointed king over Israel. He was not anointed by Samuel to be king "one day" in the future. He was anointed king at that moment. He was the true king from the second the oil was poured on his head; but instead of seeing himself as royalty, he went back to his sheep! David was a shepherd.

Shepherds can become kings, but kings hardly ever become shepherds.

Shepherds can become kings, but kings hardly ever become shepherds.

Long before Goliath, David had already won many battles. Scripture tells us that he killed a bear, and even a lion, in the wilderness when they tried to attack his sheep. So Goliath was not a big deal to him. He had already seen what God could do through him in battle.

David was a true shepherd. In fact, the whole battle of David and Goliath was birthed in the heart of a teenage shepherd. The people of God were the sheep of the Chief Shepherd (God). David understood this clearly. He saw God in a way that most could not. In fact, he would later write a song about it. You may have heard it a few times: "The Lord is my Shepherd, I shall not want" (Psalm 23:1).

So when David heard Goliath railing insults against the people of God, he took it personal. It was an assault against the sheep of the Chief Shepherd. His mind went back to the lion and bear and said, "This Philistine is no different than one of those animals." With one stone and a slingshot, the giant came down. The people were amazed; David was not.

He became famous in an instant. As we have discussed earlier, this spawned extreme jealousy in the heart of King Saul. In the end, it would lead to the downfall of Saul and his kingdom. David would eventually become the "official" king. The shepherd boy would sit on a golden throne in a palace covered in gold.

It was a long way from the isolation of the wilderness, with only a few sheep to hear him play his harp, to the king's palace. He was now surrounded by servants, beautiful women, and all the luxuries of life.

We don't know exactly when it began, but at some point the palace became more important to David than the people. He had always been able to process the praises of the people, without allowing that to prevent him from pursuing his purpose—but something had changed.

David decided to rest. He had convinced himself that he had fought enough bears and lions. He deserved a break. After all, he killed Goliath. He was a legend. I'm sure David thought he was still the same man, but the truth was he had been on a slow fade. Gone was the ruddy boy from the fields. He was now a polished, manicured, and perfumed king, surrounded by a lavish lifestyle none of his fellow shepherds and friends would ever know.

But David was also a warrior! He had fought many battles over the years as he prepared and waited for his opportunity to be king. But something had changed over time.

"It happened in the spring of the year, at the time when kings go out to battle, that David sent Joab and his servants with him, and all Israel; and they destroyed the people of Ammon and besieged Rabbah. But David remained at Jerusalem" (2 Samuel 11:1).

As king, he had led many battles. Now he felt like he had "paid his dues." He could just send the others to fight while he stayed at home to "rest." It was a trick of the Enemy to slow the momentum that had driven him his entire life. The slow fade is very deceiving.

The Enemy works this way because he knows we slowly deteriorate into another person over time—one we never dreamed we could become. If it happened fast, we would probably recognize it. But the slow fade is fueled by denial. We don't think anything has really changed. We believe we are still the same person.

The Enemy works this way because he knows we slowly deteriorate into another person over time—one we never dreamed we could become.

One day, while all his friends were in battle, David decided to go up on the roof of his mighty palace. He knew that all the men were gone, and all the wives were alone in their homes.

There was one particular woman that David was watching as she was bathing on her rooftop. Her name was Bathsheba. She was not worried about anyone watching her because she assumed all the men of the city (and even the palace) were in battle. They all were—except one: David.

The "man after God's own heart" began to lust after another man's wife. He felt entitled to her. He was the king. He was the man. So he called for her and she came. What was she going to say? He was the king.

He had intimate relations with her and committed adultery. Not long after that, she realized she was pregnant. There was no doubt that the baby belonged to David. Her husband, Uriah, had been in battle when she would have conceived.

Pride and arrogance will cause you to do some crazy things. David hatched a plan to bring Uriah off the battlefield so he could sleep with his wife, Bathsheba. This way, Uriah would think that the baby was his. But Uriah would not go into the house to sleep with her. He slept at the door of the king's house instead.

When David questioned him as to why he didn't go home to his wife, Uriah told him he didn't feel it was the right thing to do because all the others where in battle and sleeping in the open fields. He was a man of honor.

Finally, in a panic, David decided to set Uriah up to be killed in battle. He sent orders for him to be put on the front lines of the war so he would die quickly.

David was out of control. Gone was the shepherd of the field. He still looked like the same man. He still sounded like the same man. But he was not the same man.

I Don't Know If I'm Still in Love with You

The momentum of work was over. We were in our new building. It was incredible. God had performed so many miracles on our behalf. We knew the favor of God was on us.

But when the physical work was over, I found myself sort of lost. I didn't know what to do with myself. Over the course of time, my days changed dramatically. Gone were the twelve-hour days of labor. They were now replaced with time in the office and in front of my computer.

The lack of a father in my life had birthed a life that was lacking discipline. If I had a task that needed to be done, I would do it. Deadlines have always been great motivators for me. Without them, I always tended to move toward wasting time and losing my focus.

This is what was happening. But because it was a slow fade, I didn't see it coming.

Because of the success of our building project, several pastors began to ask me to come and speak in their churches. It was a dream of mine to travel and preach in other churches. I knew our story was powerful, and people wanted to hear about it.

It was one of these preaching engagements that God would use to shake me to the core.

I had just finished sharing a powerful message on favor that night. I had told our story about how God had come through in such a dramatic fashion at the literal last minute. The house was full of faith, and God moved greatly.

After the service, my family went to a local restaurant before going back to the hotel. My kids were sitting at another table a few feet away from Sandy and me. We ate our food and didn't really say much to each other. Without me really noticing it, this had become the norm for us. We were not talking much in those days. We were both very tired physically and emotionally. We were burnt out on many levels, but I never doubted "us." I knew the ministry was stressful to us both big-time, but it would never tear us apart.

We were God's "power team." All that we had been through together assured me that our marriage was the one area of my life that I had "locked up." Then out of nowhere, Sandy said, "I must get this off my chest." She began to weep, and then told me that she was miserable. It began to flood out of her. I couldn't believe what I was hearing. Like a skilled surgeon, she began to dissect the slow fade of her husband. She agonizingly laid out all she had been forced to see happening in my life over the past few years.

The man that she had seen "greatness" in was gone. It was painful for her to watch. It was excruciating to hear. Then came the words I never thought I would ever hear.

"Larry, I love you, but I don't know if I am 'in' love with you anymore. I want you to know that if something doesn't change by this time next year, I am leaving you. I don't want to leave. I don't know how I will make it. But I will leave. I am miserable."

I was stunned. I did not see this coming at all. There was nothing really to say, except, "I am sorry" repeatedly. That is what I did.

People saw me as a great, disciplined man of faith, but the truth was that I was the complete opposite.

She was right. My heart had changed. I had changed. I was, in many ways, a fraud—again. People saw me as a great, disciplined man of faith, but the truth was that I was the complete opposite. Somewhere along the way, I had simply "checked out" of every area of my life. I had isolated myself in my own little bubble and expected everyone in my world to be OK with that.

But there was no way I was going to lose the greatest thing to ever happen to me. I took her words to heart. I repented to my wife and to God. I said within my spirit, "I am not only going to get back to the man I was, but I am going to be a better man than I was. Somehow, I am going to find that 'greatness' again."

The year was 2006 when that dreadful conversation happened. The year 2007 was coming! Seven is the number of completion. It is the number of perfection, so I began to declare that '07 would be the greatest year of my life.

The Worst Birthday

I started preaching messages to our church about the year 2007 during the middle of 2006. We would confess together: "Next year will be the greatest year of our entire lives." As the end of the year grew closer, I could sense a renewed "momentum." It was going to be amazing. I was pumped.

We had a New Year's Eve service that year, and counted down to the "number of perfection" – '07! Sandy and I were on the stage together when the year began. You could feel it. I was back. We were back. Momentum! Personally, I was especially excited that the seventh day of 2007 fell on a Sunday. It was perfect. I would be preaching on the seventh day of the seventh year of a new millennium. It couldn't get any better.

I preached with fire that day. I made many proclamations over my life and the church. We even planned for a huge outdoor event on July 7, 2007. It would be 7-7-7. As you can see, I was "all in" on this being the "greatest year of my life."

But remember, emotional momentum is mythical. It is not real (in tangible form). It can trick you. That night, I went home exhausted. To use a sports analogy, I had "left it all on the field." I had preached my heart out, and I couldn't wait to get to my recliner and crash! I did just that. I was relaxing in my chair, drinking some amazing sweet tea, while I watched television. I looked down at my watch, and I noticed that it was a little after 7 p.m. on January the seventh of 2007.

Then something happened that would instantly set into motion a series of events that would almost kill me several times. Pain like nothing I had ever experienced in my life hit my side. I fell out of my chair and collapsed on the floor. I was alone. Everyone in my family was asleep in various parts of the house. I cried out for help, but no one could hear me. I didn't know what was happening.

Eventually I got Sandy's attention, and she rushed to help me. Neither one of us knew what was going on. I thought I might have eaten something that was upsetting my stomach really bad. I assured her I would be OK. We prayed, and I told her to just go to bed. I was going to stay downstairs until I felt better.

The pain grew stronger as the night went on. I was convulsing in pain. Sometime around 2 a.m., I knew that I was probably going to have to go to the hospital. Even so, I decided to push through until it was the normal time for everyone to get up that morning.

Once everyone was awake, Sandy realized how bad it was. I was a mess. It was my birthday. I was thirty-nine years old that day. What a birthday it was starting out to be. Instead of cake, the movies or dinner, I was headed to the emergency room.

Behold! You Are the Man

David had fallen greatly from the young man he was on the day of the prophet Samuel's visit. A lot of water had gone under the bridge since then. Gone were the days of fighting for the sheep and soothing their wounds around the campfire at night. The shepherd seemed to have vanished into the prestige of the palace.

David never wanted to be king. He was a servant above all else. Even when he was already anointed king of Israel, he continued to serve King Saul. This was the heart of a shepherd. This passion to serve the people of God is what would cause God to say of him, "I have found David, the son of Jesse, a man after My own heart" (Acts 13:22).

What is God's heart? The sheep! As long as David flowed in the heart of the shepherd and put others before himself, God was pleased. But along the way, David lost his focus.

He was now sitting in the palace, knowing that he had betrayed one of his most loyal soldiers and friends. He had committed adultery with Bathsheba, and now she was pregnant with his child. Then he had devised a plan to have Uriah killed in battle before he could ever know of her pregnancy and of his disloyalty.

When a person is in a place of arrogance and pride, it will always breed an attitude of entitlement. You will convince yourself that it is OK. You are the man. You deserve to have whatever your heart desires. You have paid the price.

Without hesitation, you will begin to defend your actions and devise plans to cover up your deeds. After all, it is really no one's business. You can deal with the issues behind the scene. No one needs to be bothered with this. You have it all under control.

When a person is in a place of arrogance and pride, it will always breed an attitude of entitlement.

When the news arrived that Uriah was dead, David felt a small sense of relief. Now he could go public with his desire to be with Bathsheba. She was available to the king. Her husband had been killed in battle. It was still early enough in the pregnancy that he could probably get away with making everyone think that it didn't happen until Uriah was dead. David had covered his tracks. Once again, he was the victor!

But God is never in the dark. Father God is never tricked or misled. He sees all things and knows all things. He was about to have an epic encounter with the former shepherd boy. The hotshot know-it-all king was about to have a rude awakening.

One day while he was sitting on the throne, being fed grapes and receiving the royal treatment, the prophet Nathan approached him. Of course, the prophets had free rein to come before King David.

When David saw Nathan, he gave him the approval to approach the throne. "What is it you need from the king today, O prophet?" the king exclaimed. Nathan replied, "I just want to tell you a story…"

The Bible records this conversation. "There were two men in a certain town. One was rich, and one was poor. The rich man owned a great many sheep and cattle. The poor man owned nothing but one little lamb he had bought. He raised that little lamb, and it grew up with his children. It ate from the man's own plate and drank from his cup. He cuddled it in his arms like a baby daughter. One day a guest arrived at the home of the rich man. But instead of killing an animal from his own flock or herd, he took the poor man's lamb and killed it and prepared it for his guest" (2 Samuel 12:1–4 NLT).

David heard this story and became enraged. He leapt to his feet and proclaimed, "Who is this man? Whoever he is, today he will be immediately put to death. He will also repay the man he stole from four times!" (2 Samuel 12:5–6, author's paraphrase).

David probably drew his sword at that very moment. He was ready to mount his horse and go through the villages until he found this horrible man. He thought: *Who could do such a thing? This is so cruel. It goes against everything we stand for in my kingdom.*

He demanded to know. "Who is the man? I need to find him and kill him. According to the Law, he has sealed his fate!"

Nathan quickly replied, "You are the man! Thus says the Lord God of Israel" (2 Samuel 12:7).

It was at that moment the running ended. I truly believe it was a huge relief for David. He was glad to be caught. He had become so brazen that whether he realized it or not, he had been escalating his actions and hoping to get caught.

He knew what Nathan had said was true. He was guilty of all of it. Finally, he was broken. Finally, someone held him accountable. Finally, he could be the shepherd again. His mind went back to the days of lions and bears and giants. He had flashes of the oil being poured on his head and hearing the words of the prophet spoken over his life.

He wondered: *How did I get here? How could I have let this happen? I'm guilty. I deserve to die!* And then he did something that probably saved his life. He cried out to God and admitted his sin.

"So David said to Nathan, 'I have sinned against the Lord'" (2 Samuel 12:13). And then he fell to his knees, ripped his outer garments (to show his brokenness), and cried out to God for healing and restoration.

Not only did the shepherd rise within him, but so did the psalmist. The broken heart of a prideful man began to sing a song of repentance and restoration. Psalm 51 records his entire prayer/song before God and the prophet. I encourage you to read the entire chapter. It is filled with some of the purest words of repentance ever recorded as well as a revelation of the restorative power of God. But there is one part of Psalm 51 that sticks out to me more than all the rest.

"Create in me a clean heart, O God, and renew a steadfast spirit within me. Do not cast me away from Your presence, and do not take Your Holy Spirit from me. Restore to me the joy of Your salvation, and uphold me by Your generous Spirit" (Psalm 51:10–12).

The broken heart of a prideful man began to sing a song of repentance and restoration.

David knew it was a matter of the heart. He knew he needed a clean heart. The shepherd cried out, "Restore to me the joy of Your salvation." He remembered when it wasn't a struggle to serve God. It was a joy.

King David had seen firsthand what it looked like for the Lord to take His Spirit from a king. He had watched Saul slowly slip into a demonic torment and rage that would eventually cost him his life and kingdom.

Thank God that repentance has always moved the heart of our heavenly Father. The prophet said, "The Lord has forgiven your sin and you will not die!" (2 Samuel 12:13b, author's paraphrase). From that day forward, David set his heart toward God. He kept his heart as a shepherd first, and a king second.

Enough Poison to Kill Five Men

When I arrived at the emergency room, I could barely walk. I was screaming in pain. I had never felt pain like that in all my life.

When they finally took me back, they did a litany of tests: X-ray, upper GI, and a few others. When it was all said and done, they sent me home with a diagnosis of "stomach acid." I was written a prescription for heartburn. I figured they must have known what they were doing.

When I arrived back at our home, I just got sicker. For several days, I ran a consistent fever. Sandy kept giving me pain relievers which should have also helped with the fever. But the fever never broke.

Several days passed, and the hospital called to check on me. When Sandy told them how I was still in constant pain and fever, they scheduled me to have my gallbladder tested. They thought that might be the issue. After ten days of suffering, I went in to have the test on my gallbladder. As soon as they injected the dye into me, I screamed. They decided it must be my gallbladder, and scheduled my one-day outpatient surgery in three days.

Thirteen days had passed since I first went to the emergency room on the morning of my birthday. I was still in pain, but I was elated to finally get this "thing" out of me so I could go on with my life. I arrived early that morning, checked in, and was quickly placed in a small room to await the physician. It wasn't long before I met the man who would finally bring me some relief. But he had something else in mind.

The doctor looked at me and asked, "In all that you have gone through, has anyone done a CAT scan on your abdomen?" I told him, "I don't think so." He replied, "Well, before I touch your gallbladder, I need to see this scan. You should not be dealing with this kind of prolonged fever." I didn't care one way or the other. I was out of it. I said, "Fine. Let's do it."

I had the scan, and then they brought me back to the small holding room with my wife. We sat there for a few minutes waiting to see what was going to happen. Suddenly, the curtain flew back and the doctor said these words, "Mrs. Ragland, I want you to know we are taking your husband to emergency surgery. We are not touching his gallbladder. Your husband's appendix has completely ruptured, and it is a mess. I don't know how long it will be. I don't have time to talk to you. We are taking him now."

The next thing I knew, they were wheeling me down a hallway, and I heard someone say, "Mr. Ragland, I'm going to give you something to put you to sleep now." That's the last thing I remember until I woke up in a recovery room, gagging. I was in an incredible amount of pain, and I couldn't move. I didn't know what had happened. I was still out of it, but I knew something major had happened to me.

It would be several more hours until I could have a conversation with Sandy. She told me what the doctor said after my surgery. It was truly shocking.

"Mrs. Ragland, your husband's appendix was the worst I have ever seen in my career. For the first time ever, I called another physician in to help me. We dug around inside him, trying to find that Mr. Ragland ever had an appendix. It was completely melted and gone. Mrs. Ragland, I think your husband will be OK, but you need to know he probably had enough poison and infection in his body to have already killed five men. He will probably be back in the hospital several times due to infections that are attacking his body. It is going to be a long road."

The greatest year of my life had just turned into a nightmare.

The greatest year of my life had just turned into a nightmare. I would go on to be in the hospital on five separate occasions in the first six months of that year. Eight days on one trip; five days on another; three or four days on others. I would lay there in the bed, being pumped full of the most powerful antibiotics made. They were trying to help my body fight an infection that could have (and should have) killed me many times over.

It seemed like it couldn't get any worse, but it was only just beginning. I was under attack. The Enemy (Satan) was determined to take me out.

I Want to Be Known in Hell

I didn't know it at the time, but the slow fade had taken a toll on my spirit, soul, and body. I was tired on every level. Now I was battling sickness and pain like I had never known.

How could this be? I was God's man! I had a vision. I had a purpose and destiny. I was a "faith man." It almost seemed as if the foundations of what I believed were being chipped away piece by piece. The Devil tried to kill my body, but I survived that round. I was not aware of how many more waves of assault were coming. I just knew that he was determined to end me, once and for all.

Satan knows that even if he can't "kill you" physically, he can wear you down over time until you become completely ineffective in life and ministry. I will give Satan one statement of credit. He is persistent. His ultimate goal is to kill you. But if he can't kill you in body, he will not stop until he has successfully destroyed your faith in God. His ultimate prize would be to render you useless to the Great Commission of the gospel.

I never dreamed I would fade to a place in which I was on the verge of shaking my fist at God. But that is where I was headed. It was about to get even worse.

Satan's goal is to kill you and your testimony, but God will use any situation to perform the opposite. His desire is to give you life and to enhance your testimony. The problem is that mankind has always been determined to learn the lessons of life the "hard way." God will let you walk down that path. He allows us to make our choices. He doesn't leave us when we make a wrong decision. Horrible times of pain, suffering, and even sickness can be used by God to shake us to the core. He doesn't do those things, but He can use anything to point us back to him.

Satan's goal is to kill you and your testimony, but God will use any situation to perform the opposite.

You may be at a place of complete confusion. You probably have thought: *How could God have allowed this to happen to me? I thought He loved me and would never leave me!*

He has not left you. You are simply a target of an Enemy who hates you. I remember hearing the old-time preachers say, "If you are not going through something today, run to these altars and get right with God! You must not be making the Devil mad!"

It may sound "old-school" to say that; but it was true then, and it is true now.

One of the reasons I was under such attack in my body was because of the vision God had put in my heart for the kingdom! I knew God had called me to do something big for Him. I didn't know what it was specifically, but I can assure you of the one thing I did know: He called me to shake up the kingdom of darkness.

When you are shaking hell, Satan takes notice. The bull's-eye attacks from the Enemy will come from all sides. But that's OK. Just try to find the strength to weather the storm. The next time you are complaining about being under assault, turn it into rejoicing because you must be shaking the gates of hell.

I want the Devil to know my name. I want hell to know my name.

I have made this statement to my church on many occasions. I live by this: "It is one thing for a believer to be known in heaven (all Christians are known in heaven). It is an entirely different thing to be known in hell." I want the Devil to know my name. I want hell to know my name.

If there was ever any doubt that Satan knew my name and wanted me to be taken out before this, it was about to be removed. Satan painted a target on me and made it clear that he knew me! My slow fade was about to be turned into a rushing river of suffering and pain. But God…

Chapter Nine

Double Jubilee

Sometimes You Must "Self-Diagnose"

After a couple of months of dealing with all of this, I began to develop massive abdominal pain again. It grew to be more painful than the ordeal of a ruptured appendix. Every day the pain would intensify and come in waves. When they would hit me, I would literally fall on the floor and scream in agony. No medicine (even prescription!) could touch the pain.

I believed I had a blockage in my intestines. I went to doctors, and they ran multiple tests. They said that I did not have any obstruction anywhere that they could see. But I knew better. I could feel it on the inside of me.

After another week of excruciating pain, I collapsed in my office. I was alone, but I knew I had to get to the hospital. I didn't have time to wait for anyone. Without thinking about what could have happened, I got in the car and drove myself to the hospital. The pains would come in waves. I would cry out for God to help me. I was sobbing and praying all the way.

When I arrived at the hospital, I went straight to the office of the doctor who had declared me free of any blockage. The receptionist told me that he was not available at that moment. She asked me to sit and wait for him to finish what he was doing, and then he would come and see me.

I sprang to my feet and said, "I am not waiting. I am dying." I went down the hallway and searched for him. I found him sitting at his desk in his personal office. I opened the door and said, "I have a blockage. I am dying. Are you going to help me?"

At that precise moment, the biggest pain yet hit me. I screamed and fell right next to his desk. He saw the seriousness of the situation and called for help. He did another test, and then came back to me and apologized. He said, "Mr. Ragland, you are correct. You have a blockage."

After further examination that day, it was determined that two feet of my colon and two feet of my small intestine was completely dead. They had both dried up due to the attack of the infection. I was rushed to emergency surgery, and the two sections were removed completely and sewn back together. I woke up in intensive care.

The healing was much slower this time.

Up in Smoke!

After several months, I finally began to feel better. It seemed the infection was gone, and the blockage was gone, too. I was sore, but not in any pain like before. I could see the light at the end of the tunnel.

Frankly, I had long abandoned the mantra of '07 being the greatest year of my life. I was now just thankful that I might be able to survive it. Then the next wave of attack against me and my family began.

I was sitting in my small office in the back of our church when I heard loud thunder. I knew it was supposed to storm that day, but I thought it was supposed to begin a lot later in the evening. We had planned on finishing our work and going home to be with the kids when they got off the bus from school.

We turned on the local news. The meteorologists were live in the newsroom. They were talking about a "wall cloud" and a possible strong tornado that had sprung up out of nowhere. They had the map of our state on the screen. The weatherman said, "In ten to fifteen minutes it will cross this highway at this point. If you live near this area, go to your safe place now!"

We both panicked because the arrow was going right through my house! I jumped in the car and headed to our home. I am sure I broke several traffic laws that day, but I knew my kids had just gotten home and were probably very scared.

As I was about a mile from my home, my heart sank. I was driving into one of the darkest and scariest wall clouds I had ever seen. I began to pray out loud and plead the blood of Jesus over my children! Moments later, I arrived.

I ran in the house screaming for the kids, but there was no response. The back door was wide open, but there was no sign of the kids. I ran outside and yelled both their names. It was then that I heard my oldest screaming. I looked at her, asking, "What is wrong? What are you saying? Why are you out here? Get in the house! A storm is coming!"

She screamed again. But this time I understood her. "Get out of the house, Daddy!" I yelled back "Why? What are you talking about?" Sobbing and shaking, she shouted, "The house is on fire!"

Sobbing and shaking, she shouted, "The house is on fire!"

I froze, and then I slowly turned around and looked back into the kitchen. I could see smoke pouring out of all sides of the door going to the basement. I had almost opened that door when I came in the house, but when I saw the back door open I hadn't touched it.

I ran to her in the yard, but then I quickly realized her sister was not with her. "Where is your sister? Please tell me she is not in the house!" She replied, "She is not in the house. She was scared and ran. I think she may be at the neighbor's house."

There was a barbed wire fence that separated our property from our neighbor's. I ran with full speed towards that fence, and with pure adrenaline I never stopped. I hopped over the fence and kept running. I saw my youngest daughter and found out that she was OK.

The storm had passed by then, but it was messing with my cell phone coverage. I was having a tough time getting through to Sandy, or even 911. Through the brokenness of the signal, Sandy thought I said to her, "The tornado hit the house, and it is all gone!" But what I was trying to say to her was, "It looks like it is going to burn to the ground."

Once the fire department arrived, they went into the basement and put out the fire. But by that time, the floors above the basement had burned through and smoke had destroyed the whole house. I thought it was a total loss. We were finally able to settle down and ask the kids what had happened. They had simply done what we had trained them to do.

They heard the weatherman say go to your safe place. That was our basement. They went down there and did exactly what they were supposed to do. Then the power went out, so they were in total darkness. We had emergency candles, and my daughter lit one so they could see.

To this day, we still don't know what happened after that. Somehow the candle flamed up and ignited some other items on the shelf, and the fire just blew up in their faces. It broke my heart to hear them tell how they were trying to put it out, but it just kept growing. They finally realized they had to get out of the house, so they ran. Thank God they ran!

"Hello, This Is Pastor Job Speaking!"

Have you ever been at a place in your life when you had to laugh to keep from crying, or even losing your mind? That is exactly how I felt the day our house burned. After all I had been through with my health, church, and marriage—now this? Are you serious? Now I don't even have my home? My kids do not have a bed to sleep in?

As I stood there, watching the fire department go throughout the remaining parts of my home and inspect it, I just started laughing. Honestly, I probably looked like a crazy man. I was laughing and crying, and crying and laughing. Then my phone rang.

I was still laughing when I said, "Hello, this is Pastor Job [as in Job in the Bible], can I help you?" The person on the other end said, "Uh, I must have the wrong number." To which I replied, "Oh, no—you got Pastor Larry, but today I am convinced I am living under the spirit of Job."

Faithfulness Doesn't Exempt You

Many people have heard about Job in the Bible. Quite frankly, most of them have never read his story or know the details of how it ended. What they do know is that his name is synonymous with suffering, loss, and rejection. The name of Job should be so much more than that.

It's true that his story is one of great loss, but it is also a story of great restoration. In many ways, it is a microcosm of humanity and the things we all go through on various levels throughout our life.

Most scholars believe Job is the oldest book in the Bible. Think about that. The first book of our Bible that was put in written form and preserved over thousands of years was a story of loss, brokenness, and restoration. God doesn't do anything by chance. This is not a coincidence. I believe Job is a strategic book for every believer.

It is also a tough book for most Christians to read and study. We do not want to read about suffering, pain, doubt, and struggle. We would much prefer to read about blessings, favor, joy, and everything working to our good.

Through the course of my life, I have come to believe that all people will go through times of testing, trial, and even suffering. I also believe that it is unscriptural for a believer to judge someone for their suffering. We have no right to equate someone's tragedy or sickness with how we think they should have responded to a situation.

Our time in the ditch can teach us compassion in a way that a blessing never could.

Believers are not exempt from suffering. God does not cause tragedy to befall us so that we will stay humble. No, the Enemy desires to "steal, kill, and destroy" us (see John 10:10). Regardless, our personal tragedies can be moments of clarity for us. Our time in the ditch can teach us compassion in a way that a blessing never could. Honestly, this is one of the ways we begin to understand how to help people in their life. It is also in these times that we learn how closely God wants to be involved in every aspect of our lives. The good and the bad. He truly is good, all the time. All the time, He is good!

Job was a true man of God. Just look at how the Bible describes him: "There was a man in the land of Uz, whose name was Job; and that man was blameless and upright, and one who feared God and shunned evil" (Job 1:1).

Most scholars agree that Job lived long before Moses and the Law. There were no written instructions for Job to follow. He didn't have a

Bible or a church to attend. Job didn't have a pastor or an accountability partner. He was simply led by his spirit to serve a God he could not see.

Because of his faithfulness to God, he was richly blessed. He had seven sons and three daughters. His wealth was significant. He was living the "good life." He was probably one of the most blessed people in the world, yet he never took it for granted.

His wife and kids were not on the same spiritual level. The Bible tells us that every day he would "rise early in the morning and offer burnt offerings according to the number of them all (*his family*). For Job said, 'It may be that my sons have sinned and cursed God in their hearts.' Thus Job did regularly" (Job 1:5, insertion mine).

Have You Considered ——?

One of the main reasons faith preachers (of which I am one) tend to shy away from the book of Job is that they don't want to deal with the reality of sudden loss. They will never say this from their pulpits, but the truth is, it is not "good for business." You will always get more "shouts" when you preach about the blessings and favor of God. No one wants to give praise for the suffering and loss they may be asked to endure.

You are not defined by what "happens" to you. You are defined by how you "respond" to what happens to you!

Reality check: Suffering and loss happen to everyone at some point in their lives. Doesn't it make sense that we look at Scripture to learn how to respond to it? You are not defined by what "happens" to you. You are defined by how you "respond" to what happens to you!

Job was just going through his life the way he always had. The family had come over for a big dinner. They were all full and lying around relaxing, but Job got up and went to worship and pray. He did this for himself and for his family. He thought he was the only one involved and that no one else was there. It was just him and the altar.

But we are never alone. Not only is our heavenly Father watching us, but the Enemy is watching us, too. We do not know what made that day so special. The actual calendar date is unknown, too. Job 1 only says, "Now there was a day when the sons of God came to present themselves before the Lord, and Satan also came among them" (Job 1:6).

"Sons of God" in that verse refers to the angels of God. They were coming before the Lord, and receiving their orders, and giving reports to God.

Satan is a fallen angel that was cast out of the actual place of heaven (where God's throne is). Although he is banned from the literal heaven, he still has access to the other two heavens. Let me explain.

There are three heavens mentioned in Scripture. The first is the atmospheric heaven (our atmosphere on Earth; the sky). The second is the celestial heaven (our solar system, the Milky Way galaxy, and all the other galaxies). The third is the planet of Heaven (the actual dwelling place of God).

Lucifer is not omnipresent like God. He cannot be everywhere at the same time. He can only be in one place. Job gives us a glimpse of where Satan spends most of his time. He is constantly going back and forth between the first and the second heavens.

He does this because he is constantly "accusing" God's prized creation (mankind) in the midst of the other angels. Scripture supports this. "Then I heard a loud voice saying in heaven, 'Now salvation, and strength, and the kingdom of our God, and the power of His Christ have come, for the accuser of our brethren, who accused them before our God day and night, has been cast down'" (Revelation 12:10).

Satan knows he can't defeat God, so he is constantly trying to mock those who were created in the image of God instead. He is always bringing up our mistakes. He does this because he hates us. But the real reason is that he hates God.

On this particular day, he was railing and accusing everyone on the earth about how they had all abandoned God. Then the Lord asked Satan a question: "From where do you come?" (Job 1:7a). Satan replied, "From going to and fro on the earth, and from walking back and forth on it" (Job 1:7b).

God knew what he meant. He was mocking our Creator directly by saying, "I've gone all over the world looking at your prized creation, and they have all turned their backs on You!" What God does next is the very reason most preachers shy away from this book.

"Then the Lord said to Satan, 'Have you considered My servant Job, that there is none like him on the earth, a blameless and upright man, one who fears God and shuns evil?'" (Job 1:8).

Job was completely unaware that this conversation was even happening. He was going about his life, thinking everything was normal. Meanwhile, there was a heavenly conversation going on at that moment that would shake his world to the ground. He was about to be tested on levels he never dreamed he would face.

For most people, the hardest part of this story is that it all began with the words of God! He bragged on Job and brought his name up. It was as if He were saying, "I've heard you tear down Jimmy and Johnny. I heard you mention Suzy and Linda. But, for some odd reason, you have not mentioned Job. Why not?"

Satan knew he couldn't mention Job because he was a man of faithfulness and favor. He had not abandoned God.

God will use anything for His glory!
He knows me better than I know myself.
He knows what I can handle,
and He wants the best for me.

I know this is a hard pill to swallow, but I have learned through my journey that God will use anything for His glory! He knows me better than I know myself. He knows what I can handle, and He wants the best for me.

We are his hands and feet. Sometimes He brings our name up and sets things in to motion that seem to be for our destruction; but if we are faithful to the end, we will always see it was for our advancement and for the advancement of His kingdom.

Thirty-One Days Straight

Due to the house fire, we would be out of our house for almost five months while they rebuilt it.

A few weeks after the fire, I begin to get sick again. By this time, I was an expert on my pain, and I knew what infection felt like. It was time for me to "self-diagnose" again. I was confident another round of infection had begun in my body.

After a doctor's visit and X-ray, it was determined something traumatic had happened when I jumped the barbed wire fence. I had ripped a fistula (or tiny hole) in the area where they had stitched my colon back together. That meant that from the moment of the fire until then, I had been leaking bile (poison) into my body. It had puddled in a section of my abdomen and was surrounding the organs in my lower body.

My doctor admitted me to the hospital and inserted a drainage tube in the area of the collected poison. He said he felt it would be drained and healed in a couple of days. "A couple of days" turned into thirty-one days straight in the hospital.

To make it even worse, I was not allowed any food, water, or even ice. I couldn't even have a wet sponge touch my lips. For thirty-one days, they fed me through a "central line" that was inserted into my neck.

Thirty-one days straight in the hospital.

During this time, my wife experienced more stress than at any other time in her entire life. She was taking care of our two children away from our home and running the church on every level. She was also meeting with contractors, and picking out carpet and tile, as they rebuilt our burned-out home. I was not there to help her with any of it.

There were some nights that she would bring the tile and carpet samples to my hospital room and lay them out for us to choose. She was incredible. All of this was happening within the year in which she had decided to leave me if things didn't change. I am sure this was not the change she was looking for.

As the days ticked by, I became more irritable. She would later tell me that it was becoming hard for her to come and see me during these long days in the hospital. I was bitter and zoned out on pain medicine. The man of faith who had stood strong with bankers and lawyers and had faith that God could do anything had been reduced to much less of that man. I truly felt like I was going through a modern-day version of Job.

Great Loss—Great Recovery

Satan responded to God's suggestion of Job with, "He only serves you because you bless him, and you have put a hedge of protection around him so that he can't be touched!" He continued, "If you removed that protection, and allowed me to destroy his blessings, I know he would curse you to your face!" God replied, "OK, I am allowing it, but you cannot touch his body" (see Job 1:9–12, author's paraphrase).

Satan unleashed an attack against everything that Job loved and possessed.

All of his children were eating dinner at the eldest son's house. While they were eating, an enemy tribe came in, stole all of his animals, and killed the servants watching them. Then a strong wind blew, and it collapsed the roof on the eldest son's home. This killed all of his sons and daughters.

Just imagine this. Because of Satan's barrage against the house of Job, he lost everything in one day! All his cattle, all his possessions, and—most tragically—all his children. Only his wife remained alive from his family. Gone in one day!

How would he respond? Satan stood back and watched with a grin. "Then Job arose, tore his robe, and shaved his head; and he fell to the ground and worshiped." The Word even goes on to say, "In all this Job did not sin, nor charge God with wrong" (Job 1:20, 22).

Satan is consistent. He does not give up. He is relentless in his attack against the believers of Christ.

What? How could this be? Why would anyone worship God under that kind of pain and loss? Satan was blown away. He did not expect this. This was not his plan. How could Job have not cursed God? Apparently, God really did know the heart of Job. But the story was far from over.

As we have established throughout this book, and you have experienced in your own life, Satan is consistent. He does not give up. He is relentless in his attack against the believers of Christ. He is like that leaky faucet that drips and drips and never stops.

So Satan came back to God again, railing and accusing all those who had failed the Lord. He spoke of so many names. I am sure he planned to include Job's name this time, but, with frustration, he realized he could not bring him up again! So once again, God does it for him.

"Then the Lord said to Satan, "Have you considered My servant Job, that there is none like him on the earth, a blameless and upright man, one who fears God and shuns evil? And still he holds fast to his integrity, although you incited Me against him, to destroy him without cause" (Job 2:3).

Satan responded in typical fashion. "Yeah, yeah, whatever. Humans only care for themselves. Job didn't curse you because all that I did was to others and not to him. If you allow me to attack his body, he will surely curse you and reject you. I will prove to you that he is not who you think he is" (Job 2:4, my paraphrase).

So God released Satan to attack the body of Job, but he made sure Satan understood that he would not be allowed to take his life. Satan attacked Job with sores and boils. They covered his body from the top of his head to the bottom of his feet. No one had ever looked or felt like that. Job was in agonizing pain.

A man who was blessed greater than any other man on the planet was now sitting in a pile of ashes and scraping the sores of his body with pieces of pottery. He had once been a beacon in his village, and now he had become an embarrassment.

But Job's heart lifted. He saw his wife coming towards him. The love of his life would bring words of encouragement. Maybe she would worship God with him and bring him a little joy in his time of suffering. He looked up at her, awaiting her words. She stared at him and said, "Do you still hold fast to your integrity? Curse God and die!" (Job 2:9).

Wow! The only family member Job had left just told him to throw it all away: to curse God and die! But look at Job's response to her: "Shall we indeed accept good from God, and shall we not accept adversity?" (Job 2:10).

Scripture continues to say that after all he had lost and all the pain of his infirmity, "Job did not sin with his lips" (Job 2:10).

After a lengthy period of suffering and waiting, it all began to take a toll on Job. He ended up cursing the day he was born. He was only human. He began to complain and hope for death. In his mind, death would be so much easier than life.

Later in the journey, God came to Job and revealed Himself. He put Job's life in perspective, as He compared it with His own master plan. God reminded Job that the world did not revolve around him. God explained how He was intimately involved in every detail of creation and existence. In the end, Job humbled himself before God and cried out in total submission.

The final chapters of the book of Job tell us this: "Now the Lord blessed the latter days of Job more than his beginning; for he had fourteen thousand sheep, six thousand camels, one thousand yoke of oxen, and one thousand female donkeys. He also had seven sons and three daughters ... In all the land were found no women so beautiful as the daughters of Job; and their father gave them an inheritance among their brothers. After this Job lived one hundred and forty years, and saw his children and grandchildren for four generations. So Job died, old and full of days" (Job 42:12–16).

The same number of children he lost is the same number that were restored to him. All his cattle were replenished, and even increased. His riches were returned on such a level that he could leave an inheritance to all ten of his kids. He died a happy father and grandfather, and he enjoyed life with four generations.

I am sure Satan never wanted to hear the name Job again!

Remember, it is one thing to be known in heaven (which Job certainly was), but it is another thing to be known in hell. Job was known in hell, but he was also personally known by Satan himself. When you live a life of greatness in the kingdom, you will be known by Satan. He will do everything in his power to destroy you! But remember, God is your Protector. He knows everything you are going through. He is the Big Picture. He wants us to be part of His Big Picture, too.

It is hard, but many times the only way we can see what God is doing is by looking in the rearview mirror after we have come out of it. I know this from personal experience.

When you live a life of greatness in the kingdom, you will be known by Satan. He will do everything in his power to destroy you!

The Day That Changed Everything

Twenty-eight days into the thirty-one days of my hospital stay was Memorial Day. I had told Sandy to not bother coming to see me. I wanted her to take the kids swimming that day and have some fun.

I was having a major pity party in my room. I felt alone and abandoned. For the first time in my ministry, I felt like God had forsaken me. It only went to the next level when Sandy called me from the side of the pool.

I could hear the kids laughing and playing in the water. I heard one of them yell my name: "Daddy, when are you coming home?" I couldn't take it anymore. I told Sandy, "You guys have a wonderful time. I am very tired. I think I am going to take a nap." She said, "OK. Talk to you later."

I hung up the phone, and just stared at the wall for several minutes. I could feel my blood boiling on the inside. Then like a volcano, it came out! I exploded on God!

"God, I have given You my whole life. My wife and kids have given everything for You. We have been talked about, torn apart, and I have almost died many times. I have never questioned You through any of this. But I am being honest with You, God; I am mad at You! You have forsaken me. Why will You not heal me? I want to get out and serve You, but I can't leave this room. Why have You done this?"

If you have ever been in the hospital, you know that nurses are constantly coming in to check your vitals. This was the case for me.

They came in like clockwork. Most of the time it seemed like every fifteen to thirty minutes. But, on this day, no one came in my room for over an hour and a half. It was just me and God. And I let Him have it!

But when I had said everything I needed to say, I heard the voice of God speak clearly: "Are you finished telling me about yourself? Now, listen to me. I will tell you about you!"

It was my David and Nathan moment. All the things I had preached and taught our people to not become, I had become. Line upon line, God began to reveal the person I was to my wife, my children, my church, my city, and my God. I was ashamed. I was broken.

Like David, I cried out, "Create in me a clean heart, O God, and renew a right spirit within me." It had been a long time since I truly repented. At that moment I realized, it had taken all of this to shake me to my core.

At that moment I realized, it had taken all of this to shake me to my core.

Three days later I walked out healed, physically and spiritually. I told Sandy all that had happened. I got down on my knees and begged her to forgive me. God began to slowly put our marriage, and our lives, back together.

When New Year's Eve 2007 arrived, I told everyone what had happened. It truly was the greatest year of my life! I wouldn't change a single thing!

January 7, 2007, would become the "Greatest/Worst Day of My Life." It created "real momentum" for my marriage, my family, and our church. We were now ready for the next phase of our vision.

It was incredible how God began to restore me after that moment of true repentance. Once I was finally at a place to hear the voice of God, it changed everything for me. I would have never been able to see what I had become until the moment of total brokenness. God restored everything. My marriage, my children, my passion, my vision, and my health.

I have not had one issue with any infection or pain related to my appendix since the day I walked out of the hospital after thirty-one days.

From My Deathbed to the Nations

Fast-forward one year, and I was sitting in a church listening to people talk about my father. This was not my biological father, but the man whose name I still carry today. I never had his DNA in my body, but I always longed to simply be his son.

It was his funeral. When he died, no one told me or my brother. We found out secondhand, but that was OK. We went to the funeral out of respect, and because we didn't want anyone to think that we were still bitter and unforgiving.

As they read the names of the "survivors" (or remaining family members), my brother and I were not mentioned at all. It was a fitting microcosm of our lives. I remember hearing my brother say something like, "Well, that sort of sums it up." I said, "Yeah, but we are here, and we took the high road."

I was totally at peace. I did not sit there rejected. I didn't feel like I had been dropped. I had a Father and He was proud of me. At that moment, I realized that I was truly free. It felt amazing.

The next day, I boarded a plane and flew to the largest Muslim nation in the world: Indonesia. I preached before thousands and told the story of my sickness and near death. I watched hundreds of Indonesian people raise their hands to accept Christ because of my story!

Devil, you are a liar! God was already using my brokenness and restoration to shake the nations.

5050 Vision (the Double Jubilee)

Since then, I can't even describe all that the Lord has done in my life. I am fully free from my past hurts and insecurities. Do I still have to deal with the emotions of my past? Of course. I will carry those scars to my grave. But I am free.

I have no hatred, or even hard feelings, against either of my fathers. I moved on from that a long time ago. God is my Father. He has given me great spiritual fathers in my life to mentor and nurture me as well.

Through the years following my health ordeal, the vision became even clearer. We realized the Old Rock School we had renovated would not be our permanent home. We didn't know where it would be.

One day, we were driving down the highway when Sandy said, "Pull in this parking lot. I have to tell you something." She has only done that a couple of times. I complied and said, "What is it?" We were sitting in the parking lot of a huge church. The largest structure in our area. She said, "God has told me that this is going to be our next building!" I was shocked. The building was not even for sale. I knew the pastor. There was still a church having services there.

I said, "Sandy, I know you hear from God, but I am not going to pray against another man's vision. I'm sorry, I can't pray for this building. It is not for sale." She answered me back, "I know. I am not saying when. It may be several years from now. But I know what I heard." Over the years, I have learned to listen to my wife when she says God is speaking! So I shelved it and kept it to myself.

Just a few weeks later, we were working on a joint community project with several other churches. One of the churches was the church that Sandy had shown me. After we were all finished working that day, a few of us pastors were standing in the parking lot, talking. The pastor of the building that God had told my wife would be ours one day approached me. He said, "I need to tell you something." I replied, "OK, what is it?" He said, "I think God is telling me, you should buy my building!"

I was stunned. My heart was racing. After several minutes of conversation, I confessed to him what the Lord had told my wife. I told him that we were praying for wisdom, and we would never pray against another church to give up their building. He said, "You didn't say anything. I did."

The following day, we were touring the building and making videos for our elders as we prepared to talk to them about it. One day later, we met with them and told them what we were feeling. The address for the property is 5050. God spoke to me and said, "Call it '5050 Vision.'" In the Bible, 50 is the number of Jubilee. This was a time of great celebration. It was a "reset." All debts were cancelled, and everyone got a "redo." This was not just our Jubilee. This was a "Double Jubilee."

The building was almost one hundred thousand square feet and sat on eighteen acres of land. It was located on the busiest highway in our area and would enable us to grow for many years. Because of this, the price was way out of our range. But that had never stopped us before.

Every building we had ever purchased was always impossible.

Favor on the Rock

Something unique happened, and it had happened way back during the time we were worshipping in our second building. We affectionately called that church location "the little white building."

We had around thirty people in attendance on Sundays, but we had a vision. One day, Sandy and I were driving on a little country road when we noticed a pile of rocks just off the shoulder of the pavement. We pulled over, took one of the larger ones, and placed it in our trunk.

The next Sunday, I stood on that rock in our little church building and cast the vision for Solid Rock Church. Since then, that rock has followed us to every building. We have always strategically placed it near an entrance of our building.

A few days after we toured this massive facility, we snuck onto the property and placed our "special rock" in a flower bed, next to one of the front entrances. We brought a prayer team, and we walked around the whole facility and prayed. We claimed that it was done!

It took over two years of negotiations and prayer. Many times, it looked like it would not happen. Through it all, we never had a lawyer, accountant, or any professional help us. We only had God.

I sat with the bank's corporate attorneys and experts as they grilled me for information and numbers. With no formal training, I answered every question. Our numbers were shocking to them. They had not seen a church do what we had done with the number of people we have had over the years. We were a risky investment, but God's favor went before us.

In the end, even our banker couldn't believe it. The press covered the entire process. Our city and other churches in our area rejoiced with us as we closed the deal on a multimillion-dollar facility.

All the things we had dreamed would happen for us one day were now possible: schools, Bible college, mission center, youth facility, and a sanctuary to handle massive growth were all here. It was truly a miracle to see. It is still a miracle to see.

God had restored all things. We had a reset, a reboot; but I firmly believe it would have never happened without all the other things mentioned in this book. I know Satan has always wanted to take me out, but he has lost at every turn.

He wants to take you out, too.

Your journey probably looks nothing like mine. There may be some similarities, but my path will never be yours because we all have our own journey to greatness. Not our greatness, but God's greatness within us.

We all have our own journey to greatness. Not our greatness, but God's greatness within us.

I am a living, breathing example of the grace, mercy, forgiveness, and restorative power of God Almighty!

In the concluding chapter of this book, I want to share a few principles I have learned over the years. I want to help you on your path to greatness in God. I opened this book with the story of how a teenage girl, who would become my wife, changed my life with one statement. When she could have— should have—walked away, she didn't. I asked her why, and she replied, "I see greatness in you!" It saved me. I had never heard that before.

My story was possible because of Jesus, and because He used her to speak something in my life I had never heard and certainly never believed.

I want to do the same for you. The closing chapter is called, "He Sees Greatness in You!"

I will attempt to help you see what God already sees. But I want you to know that I see it in you too! Get ready! It's time for the next step, in your journey to greatness!

Chapter Ten

He Sees Greatness in You!

It Is All about Perspective

Have you ever been in a big hurry to get somewhere and realize you didn't have any time to spare? You are praying that each red light will magically become green. You probably break a few speed limits on your way while asking for forgiveness. It appears that you are going to make it. You only have one more hurdle to cross, and you will make it on time—the train tracks that you know you must cross.

Sure enough, just as you are about to cross, the lights begin to flash and the arm comes down. You are stuck. There is no way around the train. You are forced to wait.

The frustrating part about waiting at a railroad crossing is the unknown. From your perspective, you have no idea when the caboose is coming. You can't anticipate the ending. You just have to wait.

I understand this analogy will not work in all parts of the world. I live in the southern region of America. The terrain will always be different in your city and in your part of the world. The land may be very flat where you are, or you may not have a lot of trees. But in my state, we are full of small and large mountains and many trees. It is virtually impossible to ever see the end of a train in Alabama. For years, I thought that was the case for the rest of the world. All I ever knew was my world. That is, until I went on the cross-country trip with my biological father mentioned earlier in the book.

I remember one particular place in the plains of Texas. We were at a rest stop, and I was standing in the parking lot. I heard the familiar sound of a train's whistle. I turned to see something that this Alabama boy had never seen. Off in the distance was a train. It looked like a toy because it was so far away, but I could see the *entire train*. From engine to caboose, I could see it all! I was blown away. I didn't think that was possible.

It's all about your perspective, or "viewability." I could see the beginning and the end because there was nothing in my way to obstruct my view.

"I am the Alpha and the Omega, the Beginning and the End, the First and the Last" (Revelation 22:13).

We have heard that Scripture most of our lives, but it is time for you to fully understand what it means. God can see the engine *and* the caboose of your life. He certainly has seen the beginning and end of any test or trial you have had to face.

God has nothing to obstruct His view. His perspective is always clear. While we wait, He is allowing things to pass by us that were not meant for us. While we are cursing the flashing train lights for making us late, He might be protecting us from something on the other side.

God has nothing to obstruct His view.
His perspective is always clear.

"'For My thoughts are not your thoughts, nor are your ways My ways,' says the Lord" (Isaiah 55:8).

God can always see the Big Picture of every phase of your life. Our ways are not His ways. He is doing, moving, removing, adding, tearing down, and building up all the time behind the scenes. It is all for our good. It doesn't always feel that way, but it is.

I need you to get this in your spirit. The key to living a life of greatness is very simple. You have to become what I call "a Big Picture person."

Learning to Live a "Big Picture Life"

One of the most important moments of my life happened in a very unexpected place—on my lawn mower! Ironically, the lawn mower is where I get most of my sermon and series ideas. It is a time of isolation and thinking for me.

On this hot summer day, I was sort of whining and complaining to God. I was telling Him about how a particular family situation was going (as if He didn't know). I was saying things like, "How could this happen to my family? We are a family of destiny and purpose. We have sacrificed it all for you. How could this person be running from God when they have seen You do so much?"

Immediately, I heard the Lord say, "Son, you've got to start looking at your world with Big Picture eyes. Do you really think this situation is going to look like this, just five years from now?"

He began to show me how He could see the caboose of this train (moment). His viewpoint was completely unobstructed. He had already seen the end. I was challenged by God to see things "now" as they will be "when." This was only possible by deciding to see the Big Picture.

This Changes Everything

When you begin to see the Big Picture, it changes everything. You begin to finally realize what it means to "walk by faith and not by sight." People look different. You respond differently to a diagnosis from your physician. Instead of complaining about the things that are happening in your life, you praise God in the midst of the storm. Big Picture living changes how you see your world, your family, and your church.

Big Picture living changes how you see your world, your family, and your church.

Big Picture living will give you the true revelation of this truth: "And we know that all things work together for good to those who love God, to those who are the called according to His purpose" (Romans 8:28).

How in the world can sickness, pain, suffering, struggle, being knocked down, dropped, broken, or abandoned ever work to our good? When you understand Big Picture living, you know that somehow, this is working for your good.

In the Beginning

Through the Big Picture, we can see the hidden potential for greatness in everything around us. Our Creator demonstrated this at the beginning of our world.

One principle that creation teaches us is the importance of the environment. It is the source of provision and sustenance for all those who live in it.

It is very interesting that God created the water, the air (or sky), and the dirt first. Then He called the plants and animals out of those environments, thus showing us the Big Picture of creation. You cannot survive without the proper environment. A fish can only survive in water. A bird is in its element while flying. Plants need soil, and animals eat from all things that are "of the dirt." But man was a different creature altogether!

When it came time to create man, God did things a little differently. He didn't speak to the sea, the air, or the earth. He spoke to Himself!

"Then God said, 'Let Us make man in Our image, according to Our likeness; let them have dominion over the fish of the sea, over the birds of the air, and over the cattle, over all the earth and over every creeping thing that creeps on the earth.' So God created man in His own image; in the image of God He created him; male and female He created them. Then God blessed them, and God said to them, 'Be fruitful and multiply; fill the earth and subdue it; have dominion over the fish of the sea, over the birds of the air, and over every living thing that moves on the earth'" (Genesis 1:26–28).

I know the flesh of man was made from the dirt. "And the Lord God formed man of the dust of the ground." But man was only a lifeless statue until God "breathed into his nostrils the breath of life; and man became a living being" (Genesis 2:7).

What was the "breath of life"? It was the breath of God Himself. This is a powerful revelation of the Big Picture of God's plan for humanity.

Our body was formed from the earth, so the earth is the environment that sustains and satisfies our flesh. But our spirit man was formed from the heart of God, the Spirit of God. This is the reason we are in a constant battle between the flesh and the spirit. One is cursed, and one is blessed.

Little Picture living is led by the flesh. Big Picture living is led by the Spirit. Holy Spirit can see the caboose of every situation; your flesh cannot. When we are led by the Spirit, we will begin to see the "good" that can come out of any situation.

He Sees Greatness in You

The Big Picture simply means that God saw greatness in you before you were ever formed in the womb of your mother. How do I know this? Simply put, God is the Big Picture. He doesn't create a person to be small and insignificant. He has called you to greatness!

God is the Big Picture. He doesn't create a person to be small and insignificant. He has called you to greatness!

I would have never dreamed that the boy who was dropped and broken by two separate fathers would travel the world and tell the good news of the Big Picture of God's plan. But that is exactly what has happened in my life. I never imagined I'd be writing a book and telling my story, but it is happening right now.

I've seen blind eyes opened, deaf ears unstopped, the lame walk, cancerous tumors disappear, alcoholics and drug addicts instantly delivered, and atheists born again! I've preached to just one person, and I've preached to many thousands, but the message is the same wherever I go. God sees greatness in you!

I am driven to tell the world that Jesus loves them and has a purpose for their lives. He doesn't need to call anyone out of their country or culture to be used by God. He formed them there to walk in greatness—there.

Greatness is not defined as earthly success, fame, or fortune. It is seen when you have made an impact on your world for Christ and leave a legacy of greatness behind you when you are gone.

I am determined to do something great for God. I am not concerned with how many people I have on the attendance roll or the size of my church building. This kind of thinking is "Little Picture" greatness. Big Picture greatness is a spiritual life; it is not a fleshly or materialistic life.

Greatness Is Already in You

As we approach the end of this book, I must return to the beginning. In the introduction, I wrote about the DNA of greatness. I want to remind you again. This is not something you are seeking; it is already in you!

God created you in His image. Therefore, greatness is within you. He will not force it out of you. It is up to you to release it.

God created you in His image.
Therefore, greatness is within you.

There are a few things I would like to encourage you to do after finishing this book. This is not an exhaustive list of "steps to greatness." It is simply a few things I've learned over the years that have helped me live a Big Picture life. They have allowed me to move on from the pains and doubts of my past to push forward to my destiny. I hope they will help you on your journey of greatness, too.

Keys to a Life of Greatness (Big Picture Living)

"Go All In"

Simply put, greatness is never achieved or released in someone's life until they decide to go "all in." No one has ever lived a life of greatness with a half-hearted effort. I've heard it said, "You can't spell God without the word 'Go.'" This is so true. God has called you to go "all in" to the purpose for which you were created.

Matthew 28:19–20 is known as the Great Commission (or command), not the Great Suggestion! It is not optional for you to walk in greatness. You have been called to the world! Of course, that means your personal world, and the world abroad.

Some have said, "I'll stay here and take care of my own little world. Those who are called to the nations can go to the nations." No! You and

I have been called to be missionaries of the good news. We don't get to sit on the bench. When you are Big Picture, you know it is your calling as well. I've heard it said: "The mission of God is too important to leave just to missionaries."

2 Timothy 1:9 tells us that it is Jesus "who has saved us and called us with a holy calling, not according to our works, but according to His own purpose and grace which was given to us in Christ Jesus before time began."

Wow! "Before time began," we were called with a holy calling. It is time to get off the bench. You are not second or third string. You have been called to get in the game. It is time to go All IN.

"Live Your Life for Others"

A life of greatness is rooted in service to others. Jesus began His ministry by pointing out the purpose for the power of the Holy Spirit in our lives. After humbling Himself to be baptized by John in the Jordan River, the Holy Spirit came "on" Him like a dove. Jesus did this to illustrate our need for the power of God, so we could walk in greatness and see the Big Picture. He left the water and fought the Devil face-to-face. After running the Devil off, he descended the mountain and headed straight for the temple.

This was Jesus' custom. He had read in the temple many times throughout His life. He was well-known by the religious leaders. As He walked in, He was immediately handed the scroll of the prophet Isaiah. The Bible says, "He found the place where it was written."

> One of the biggest obstacles to a Big Picture life is selfishness. Get your eyes off yourself and your "issues" and put them on others.

Then he read out loud, "The Spirit of the Lord is upon Me, because He has anointed Me to preach the gospel to the poor; He has sent Me to heal the brokenhearted, to proclaim liberty to the captives and recovery of sight to the blind, to set at liberty those who are oppressed; to proclaim the acceptable year of the Lord" (Luke 4:17–19).

Jesus made it clear that His greatness and His purpose were rooted in setting the captives free and helping the hurting people. We must follow His example.

One of the biggest obstacles to a Big Picture life is selfishness. Get your eyes off yourself and your "issues" and put them on others. What you do to help others, God will do for you.

"Surround Yourself with Greatness"

Without question, this is one of the most important Big Picture life principles. People have the ability to lift you or drop you. I have been lifted and dropped by others on many occasions.

The opening chapter told the story of the first time anyone really saw greatness in me. Sandy didn't see "Larry's greatness." Sandy saw the greatness of God within me. I am nothing special. She didn't see anything in me that is not already in you. You just need someone to see it and call it out.

If no one has ever said, "I see greatness in you" to you, let me be the first. "I see greatness in you!" Even though I am not there with you, I see it in you. I know it is there. God put it there.

One of the most important things you can do on your journey is to ask God to lead you to your spiritual father or mother.

One of the most important things you can do on your journey is to ask God to lead you to your spiritual father or mother. You need a covering in your life. I'm not talking about a preacher. I am talking about a man or a woman who can see greatness in you. Someone who will cultivate that greatness and not be afraid to call you on the carpet for bad decisions. He or she will do it in love, but it must be done.

You have already proven that you are not strong enough to walk the Big Picture life on your own. In fact, you are not designed or equipped to do life alone. God has created us to need each other. Find a person or a group of people who are already walking in the anointing that you desire for yourself. Hang around them, listen to them, take notes, and even emulate the things you admire. They are not your ultimate example, but God will use the testimony of others to pull your testimony out of you.

"Don't Live in the Past, But Don't Forget It"

When most of us think of living a life of greatness for God, we usually envision a life free from the pains of our past. We have been told (rightfully so): "Therefore if the Son makes you free, you shall be free indeed" (John 8:36). Therefore, we think that means we will never have to deal with the past again.

This may be the case for some, but it was not the case for me. Yes, I am free from my past. There is no hatred, anger, bitterness, or depression left in me because of all that has happened in my life. I have endured a lot of hardship, but it has made me the man I am today.

You can't do anything about your past. What has been done, is done. Counseling is very important and essential to our healing, but we can't spend the rest of our lives lying on a couch talking about our past. At some point, we must move on. We must forgive. We will never forget, but we have got to forgive.

The reason you have a "testimony" is because you have been through a "test."

The reason you have a "testimony" is because you have been through a "test." I have said on many occasions, "If I could go back in time, I wouldn't change anything." Why? Because, the love, grace, mercy, and forgiveness I extend to others has been molded in the pain of my past.

I am the father I am today because of all that happened to me with my two fathers. When I visit someone in the hospital, my compassion is rooted in the hospital beds of 2007 when I almost died. No, God did not do any of those things; but through them, I saw more of the Big Picture heart of God than I ever had before.

When you're faced with a mountain in your life—speak to it! Tell it to go! Walk in faith. But if God asks you to climb the mountain, strap on your spiritual backpack and climb it! You will see a lot of the Big Picture from the top of those mountains! Your experience will give you a whole new perspective.

"Be Open to Loving Criticism"

One of the hardest things for a leader to receive is constructive criticism. I'm not talking about listening to someone intimidate or ridicule you. People intent on this kind of talk should be removed from a life of greatness. That's not what you need, but you do need a place in your life in which you are comfortable enough to listen to those who may not see things the same way you do.

Many great leaders and ministers have fallen because they did not allow anyone to disagree with them. Greatness is not tied to you always being right. Greatness is tied to doing the right thing!

Greatness is not tied to you always being right. Greatness is tied to doing the right thing!

Many times, our desire is to do the right thing, but we are on the wrong path. God can use others to help us change direction—if we are willing to listen. I can't tell you the times my spiritual father has said, "Now son, I hear you. You know I am for you and not against you. Am I your spiritual father? Will you listen to me? I'm not telling you what to do, but I need you to see a different angle on this." Of course, my response is always, "Yes, I will listen." Without fail, his wisdom always points me to the correct path.

Remember, it is all about perspective. You and your mentor(s) may be sitting at the same crossing, but he or she may be a little higher than you. They have lived this moment before, therefore they can see what you can't see. You need this in your life. I need this in my life.

"Be a Worker"

Many pastors, leaders, and business owners teach a concept called a pyramid hierarchy. They are trained in seminars that the first thing they should do is delegate. They think that if you are not "passing the buck," you are not leading.

I completely understand the premise and frankly, I agree with it, but I am afraid it has also created a generation of elite people "at the top" who have forgotten the reason they began the ministry or business to begin with. I'm concerned that we have raised a generation of lazy and entitled people who are now in leadership positions. They have lost their connection to the people they lead and to the mission of the organization.

I am not saying that everyone should be like me. I've always tried to lead by example. I will never ask anyone I am leading to do something that I have not, or would not, do myself. People will follow those who are not afraid to get their hands dirty.

People will follow those who are not afraid to get their hands dirty.

People are looking for leaders who smell like sheep. Shepherds smell like sheep. If you are never working with the sheep, you will not smell like the sheep. The kingdom of God is about people. The greatness within us will always lead us to helping people.

Every once in a while, get out of the office and sweat a little. Strap on a tool belt. Push a lawn mower. Do something. Work was created by God. It was not "imposed" on mankind as a curse. It was meant to be a blessing. Don't be afraid of it. Once you put the work gloves on, you get to see the rest of the Big Picture.

Leaders lead, but sometimes we just teach. When we only teach and never come out of our comfort zones, we only see part of the picture.

"Never Stop Learning"

If you are teachable, you are reachable! Never stop learning and growing. Your age, or formal education level, has nothing to do with your ability to educate yourself and grow.

This principle applies to the Word of God, but it also applies to your family and your career. God's will is for the hidden greatness within you to shine in every aspect of your life.

God's will is for the hidden greatness within you to shine in every aspect of your life.

Years ago, I met a very successful doctor. He was a millionaire and owned several businesses as well. This man had a spirit of excellence and greatness on him to which I was drawn. I wanted to listen to any advice he could give me regarding success in my own life. I asked him to tell me just one thing I could do that would make a major difference in my life. He simply said, "Larry, never stop reading."

He went on to paint a picture for me that has stuck with me for the rest of my life. I have taught this principle to many leaders, pastors, and my own team in our church.

He said, "Imagine, if you will, a giant bookshelf. It is so tall you can barely see the top shelf, but as you visualize it, I want you to notice the shiny object on the top. Larry, that bright object is your destiny. It is completely out of reach. There is no ladder in the room. There is only one way to make it to the top and reach your destiny. You must take a book off the shelf and read it. Once you finish it, sit it down on the floor and then stand on it. Pick another book, read it, and stack it on top of the last book. Throughout your life, you will climb the bookshelf. One day, you will have read enough books to reach out and grab your destiny."

Since that moment. I have never stopped reading. As long as my body and my mind will cooperate, I will continue to read. I read the Word of God first and foremost, but I also read other books that build me up and release the greatness within me. You've almost finished this book. After the final word, you will be higher on the bookshelf of your life.

No Time Like Right Now

I have taken you on a journey through my life and the lives of some of our greatest biblical heroes that ever lived. It has not been easy to tell the story of my broken past. Many nights, I cried as I was typing and reliving the pain of my childhood. The scars are still there.

For decades, I kept most of the events in this book a secret. I only allowed a handful of people to know about them. I wondered if I would ever have the courage to publicly speak about my life. Many stories were not included. There simply was not enough room in this book to tell them all.

I have purposely left all people (except my wife and pastor) unnamed. My goal was not to slander anyone or their families. But the story had to be told. Why? Because I am convinced if the greatness of God can be revealed in a life like mine, it can be revealed in any life.

I am convinced if the greatness of God can be revealed in a life like mine, it can be revealed in any life.

I am certainly not equating my life to the suffering of someone who has been sexually abused, diagnosed with a terminal illness, or raised in complete poverty. Many people have been dropped and broken in their lives by others. Many feel like they have been shafted in life. They were born into a situation in which it seems like the odds were stacked against them from birth.

But I know that God is the Big Picture, and He has not forsaken them, or you. He sees greatness in everyone. He sees greatness in you.

Take a deep breath and blow it out. Did you do it? Seriously, I need you to do it.

Did you have breath? Of course you did. That means you are alive! And if you are alive, there is greatness in you. God put it there!

It is time to rise from the ashes. It is time to get off the bench. You can't change the past, but you can change the future. You can decide to be the Big Picture. You can decide to allow the pain of your past to push you to your purpose!

Now is the time. Let this book be more than my story. Let it be your story.

It is time to rise from the ashes. It is time to get off the bench. You can't change the past, but you can change the future.

If not now, when? Now is the time for greatness!

God sees greatness in you! It's time for you to see it also. Do you see it?

About the Author

Larry Ragland has almost thirty years' experience in local church ministry. Alongside his wife, Sandy, and their two daughters, he founded Solid Rock Church in Birmingham, Alabama. Together they have pastored the same church for over twenty-five years. Larry is also an evangelist who has preached the gospel in several states and many countries. In 1996 he founded Ambassadors Bible College, which has equipped church planters, pastors, and missionaries around the world. His passion is to lead leaders and equip this generation for maximum kingdom impact.

Larry can be contacted at larry@larryragland.com.

CPSIA information can be obtained
at www.ICGtesting.com
Printed in the USA
BVHW040720120921
PP12618200001B/2

9 780692 169032